Mindset for Success

Discover the Millionaire Secrets, Habits and Highly Effective People Exercises for Self-Discipline, Use Self-Esteem and Confidence to Achieve Your Goal & Ultimate Mindfulness

by

Ernest Brown

© Copyright 2018 by Ernest Brown

All rights reserved.

The content contained within this book may not be reproduced, duplicated or transmitted without direct written permission from the author or the publisher.

Under no circumstances will any blame or legal responsibility be held against the publisher, or author, for any damages, reparation, or monetary loss due to the information contained within this book. Either directly or indirectly.

Legal Notice:

This book is copyright protected. This book is only for personal use. You cannot amend, distribute, sell, use, quote or paraphrase any part, or the content within this book, without the consent of the author or publisher.

Disclaimer Notice:

Please note the information contained within this document is for educational and entertainment purposes only. All effort has been executed to present accurate, up to date, and reliable, complete information. No warranties of any kind are declared or implied. Readers acknowledge that the author is not engaging in the rendering of legal, financial, medical or professional advice. The content within this book has been derived from various sources. Please consult a licensed professional before attempting any techniques outlined in this book.

By reading this document, the reader agrees that under no circumstances is the author responsible for any losses, direct or indirect, which are incurred as a result of the use of information contained within this document, including, but not limited to, — errors, omissions, or inaccuracies.

Table of Contents

Introduction 7

Chapter 1: Embracing the Philosophy of Growth Mindset . 9

    What is Growth Mindset 9

    How to Develop a Growth Mindset 11

Chapter 2: Avoid Distractions 20

    Why Do You Need to Avoid Distractions? 20

    How to Get Rid of Distractions? 21

Chapter 3: Stay Focused 32

    What Does the Term 'Focus' Mean? 32

    How to Achieve Focus in Your Tasks? 33

Chapter 4: Practicing Good Habits 41

    Why Is It Important to Develop Good Habits? 42

    How to Develop Good Habits? 42

Chapter 5: Appreciate Your Manifestation Power 51

    What Is the Power of Manifestation All About? 51

    How Is Gratitude Relevant for Implementing Your Manifesting Power? 52

    Swap 'I Have to' for 'I Get to' 56

    Be Grateful for the Smallest of Things 57

Working on the Power of Manifestation 58

Chapter 6: Increase and Reinforce Your Knowledge 62

How Is Increasing Knowledge Linked with the Growth Mindset? 62

How to Increase and Reinforce My Knowledge 63

Chapter 7: Stimulate Your Creative, Intuitive Mind 72

Why Do You Need to Stimulate Your Creative Mind? 72

Chapter 8: Conduct Manifestation Experiments 83

7-Step Manifestation Experiment 83

What Will You Need for This Experiment? 84

Chapter 9: Track Your Manifestation 95

Why Do You Need to Track Your Manifestation? 95

Chapter 10: Perform Active and Passive Affirmations ... 105

How to Write an Affirmation 105

How to Make Your Affirmations Work 109

Chapter 11: Self-Guided Meditations for Manifestors 115

How to Use Meditation for Achieving Your Manifestation Goals 115

Chapter 12: Build Positive Expectations 128

Building Positive Expectations 130

Positive Affirmations 131

Visualization 132

Surround Yourself with Positive People................................ 133

Devour Some Positive Mental Meals.................................... 134

Positive Training 135

Law of Attraction 136

Conclusion... 137

Introduction

Do you want to be successful in life? Do you want to achieve everything that you always wanted to? If your answers are yes, this book is exactly what you need right now! As you flip through the pages, you will find detailed insight on everything that you've ever wanted to know about being successful in life.

Whether it's embracing a growth mindset, avoiding distractions, staying focused, practicing good habits or appreciating the power of manifestation, this book will provide you with a step-by-step guide.

In this book, I have de-bunked common myths, introduced alternative approaches towards success, and added plenty of actionable goals that can be achieved by anyone. Because this isn't another superficial guide with arbitrary goals, as you read through the chapters, you will get a better grasp about the things you need to do, and a stronger idea about the things you need to avoid in order to be successful.

For my readers' benefit, I have particularly focused on the growth mindset throughout the book. This is primarily because growth mindset is imperative to your overall, holistic success. Remember, having fixed thoughts and ideas won't really take you anywhere. In order to make it big, you have to open doors for newer and out-of-the-box ideas, step out of your comfort zone, and do everything that makes you scared or afraid. It is only when you do such things that you'll truly achieve success in life.

As you flip through the chapters, you'll also notice that I've shared a couple of my personal experiences. This is because I want to make the subject easier for you to understand. I want you to understand that anyone can be successful, if they follow the right set of rules and maintain proper, consistent discipline.

While the first few chapters offer step by step guidelines on improving focus and practicing good habits, the later ones deal with more practical approaches concerning manifestation experiments, active and passive affirmations, self-guided meditation and more!

So if you're really looking to make it big in life and achieve things that are practically impossible for others, give this book a try! It'll definitely live up to your expectations!

Chapter 1: Embracing the Philosophy of Growth Mindset

Success doesn't come easy. It takes plenty of patience, lots of practice and absolute consistency. But before you embrace success, there are a couple of things that you need to do. And guess what? One of the first things you need to do is follow and adopt a growth mindset. But what exactly is a growth mindset in the first place and how are you supposed to adopt it? Well, that is exactly what we will get to learn in the following sections. In this chapter, I'll give you a detailed insight on the growth mindset. I'll also share some useful snippets of wisdom that'll help you to better embrace and adopt this mindset.

What is Growth Mindset

A growth mindset can be best defined as our inherent abilities to develop and nurture intelligence. This term dates back several years to when it was first coined by a professor of psychology, Carol Dweck. Dweck conducted research where she observed that children who assume that intelligence is acquired have better problem-solving abilities than the ones who assume intelligence is a single, inherent, fixed entity that can't be altered. People with a growth mindset believe that they can achieve anything in life with effort, proper guidance, and persistence. These individuals aren't bogged down by major or minor roadblocks as they believe in their abilities to grasp new things.

In the simplest terms, a growth mindset is the mentality that accompanies the process of growth within your brain. It is the kind of perspective that pushes you to do more. This is the mindset that is needed to 'actually' take up activities that encourage you to feel 'true growth' in your system; the kind of activities that'll trigger your growth by manipulating your neural pathways.

The mindset develops when you learn new skills, expand your horizon with your current skills and engage in new modes of activities and learning. It isn't something you inherently have, but something that you strive to achieve. It isn't something that has to be accomplished, but rather a constant process of maintenance that needs to be balanced with time. A Growth mindset won't come easily. You need to motivate yourself to the core in order to achieve it. You have to be entirely 'invested' in order to achieve it. Unmotivated actions cannot be classified as a growth mindset, because it doesn't have any scope for growth in the first place. Your growth mindset is the culmination of engaging, motivating and incredibly productive strategies that eventually go on to positively impact the neural pathways of your brain.

How to Develop a Growth Mindset

Developing a growth mindset is easier than you assume. All you have to do is follow the next couple of guidelines and be consistent with your schedule. Once you do that, you'll soon be able to follow through with everything that comes with this mindset.

Acknowledging and Embracing Your Imperfections

This is one of the most difficult and yet most important aspects of achieving a growth mindset. After all, can you ever be mindful and open to change when you're constantly finding faults with yourself and everybody else? Perhaps one of the best ways to start out with your goal is to constantly reaffirm and tell yourself that, since you're human, you are capable of making mistakes. I personally turn out to be most authentic when I am compelled to admit that I'm not aware of everything around me, and I do make some mistakes. This makes me all the more likely to embrace the imperfections in the people around me and love them despite these minor glitches.

In case you're struggling to adopt this new change, try jotting down motivational quotes in a notebook. You can also set positive reminders in your phone. For instance, if you're heading out for something as important as an interview or an exam, try setting hourly reminders that'll motivate you and remind you that you *can* make mistakes. As you see the reminders from time to time, they will automatically have a positive impact on your life.

Remember, in order to achieve a growth mindset you first have to believe in your inherent abilities. You cannot beat yourself up for everything bad that happens in your life. Understand your weaknesses and try transforming them into strengths. Most of us have the toxic tendency of looking back in the past and beating ourselves up for anything bad that happened in our lives. And this is exactly what you need to get rid of. For instance, you may not be the most structured and organized person, but that doesn't mean you're terrible at everything. If you have this weakness and understand it well, try countering it with some positive quality like flexibility. You can always be more flexible and open to possibilities despite being disorganized and messy.

Considering Your Challenges to Be New Opportunities

In life, we encounter new, challenging situations at every turn. Whether it's applying for a new position, trying a new course, or learning something different, challenges are immense, and at times, they can get quite overwhelming. But despite the overwhelming nature of these challenges, you need to accept them and make the most out of them. In fact, accepting these challenges is perhaps one of the most important aspects of developing as an individual. The more you test your limits, the more will you get to learn about yourself. New challenges aren't really a roadblock; rather, they are an opportunity to learn something new and to learn to understand yourself better.

One of the main reasons why people are afraid to accept new challenges is because they fear the possibilities of failure. All of us aren't really strong. So instead of finding opportunity in a challenge, we usually focus on the impact of failure. This mentality is the sole reason why we stumble and stutter before taking on something new. The possibilities of failure weigh us down, so we try avoiding a challenge and instead follow the same path as before. We make inane excuses in order to avoid a challenge. We do everything possible to avoid getting out of our comfort zones.

But staying in a comfort zone solely because of fear isn't as comfortable as you'd assume. By avoiding a specific challenge, you're missing out on the opportunity to learn about yourself and understand your abilities better. You'll feel perennially trapped. It's almost like you're living a life that isn't true to your own potential. Your mind is clouded by thoughts discomfort, unhappiness, anxiety, and a crippling sense that things should be different.

And this is exactly why you need to accept the challenge and try to make the most out of it. In order to lead a life of mindfulness, with a growth mindset, you'll have to accept the new challenges that come your way. After all, it is these challenges that'll give you better opportunities in helping you assume your true self. Yes, you will be afraid. You will fear stepping out of your comfort zone. But if you're really looking to grow as an individual, you'll have to rise above this fear, take the challenge, and use it to its maximum potential.

Avoiding Validation

If you're really looking to learn and grow as an individual, the first thing you need to do is avoid seeking validation. While this is easier said than done, once you achieve this, achieving a growth mindset will be easier than ever. Remember, validation can never have a positive impact on your life. It exhausts you, compels you to question yourself, and makes your life miserable.

In order to grow in life, you have to understand two things: you can't make everyone happy, and all your actions won't have the same impact on others. If you're really doing something you enjoy, why even bother about others? The more you bother, the more complicated will things be. You'll be under the pressure of unrealistic expectations and by the end of it, you won't achieve anything substantial.

One of the very steps to avoid seeking others' validation is to be aware that we, as individuals, are stuck with our own doubts, insecurities, and uncertainties. So before doing anything else, you need to understand your actions. The very idea of seeking validation from others stems from your own self-doubt. So once you're aware of how often you seek others' validation, you get a chance to start working on yourself from scratch. As you identify this glitch, you will understand yourself better. You also will develop a sense of self-worth.

Your self-worth is the understanding of the fact that you're loved by the people around you, because of your inherent abilities and not merely because of the ideas they have about you. When you tend to seek validation from others, this sense of self-worth is relatively low. So if you're really looking to develop yourself, you first need to do away with this belief.

Paying More Attention to Quality

Every time I tell someone about developing a growth mindset, I observe a weird similarity. Almost immediately after, they ask me for a timeline. As bizarre as it sounds, almost everyone wants to know how soon they should be achieving a growth mindset instead of focusing on the quality of the mindset alone. Everyone wants to grow faster than the next person. Everyone one wants to achieve the best things in life as soon as they can. And guess what? This is exactly where they are going wrong.

Developing a new mindset isn't really an easy job. You don't just wake up one morning and 'develop' the mindset. Contrarily, it is a tedious and time-consuming process that involves plenty of trial and error. You need to keep on trying and practicing things until you achieve a certain standard.

While you need to have a plan and focus on it, you can't sacrifice quality in order to grow prematurely. That doesn't help at all. You need to start everything from scratch, focus on the small, minute details and work on them individually.

Developing a growth mindset involves a lot of change. You need to change your habits, your course of action, your perceptions. And trust me, this doesn't happen overnight. You need to give yourself the time to fit into a new role. You need to give yourself the time to develop and implement a new mindset. It is only when you take your time that you end up growing and developing as an individual.

Embracing Criticism Positively

Taking criticism can be challenging, let alone learning from it. But in order to thrive and succeed, you need to embrace any criticism that comes your way. I know; some critiques can be downright toxic. But even then, you need to hear what the other person is trying to say. Don't always be defensive. When someone has a negative opinion about something you've done, hear them out first. Try to understand their perspectives.

I am not asking you to follow every criticism that comes your way. I am not asking you to go by criticism from people who are merely trying to pull you down. All I am asking is for you to hear them out. It doesn't hurt, does it? As you hear them out, you will also inadvertently develop a tolerance for hearing negative things. Right after that, you can decide which advice you want to follow and what advice you'd rather ignore. Once you start developing the habit of hearing and considering criticism, you will take a step forward in developing a growth mindset.

Setting New Goals

Learning is something that never stops, no matter what! Just because you've performed well on an exam or completed a project successfully doesn't mean you'll no longer focus on the subject. If you're really looking to achieve a growth mindset, this is one of those habits that you need to do away with. Growth-minded individuals are always on the lookout for new goals. It is these goals that keep them stimulated; it is these goals that keep them from wanting more. So once you've achieved a specific goal, try working on a new one almost immediately.

Yes, you'll obviously take your break before starting something new again. But make sure that break isn't long enough to distract you from your cause. In order to develop a growth mindset, you need to have a relentless quest for making it big. Being satisfied and drawing the line shouldn't be something that you practice doing. In case you're easily tempted or distracted, try writing down a list of goals in your notebook or online app. So every time you meet a goal, your attention is automatically diverted to the other one. When you do this from time to time, you'll develop a habit of trying to make the most of your life. And this is exactly how you'll take your final step in developing a growth mindset.

Chapter 2: Avoid Distractions

Your ability to stay focused isn't just another good habit—it is one of the most essential factors in developing a growth mindset. Remember, achieving new things is an extremely important aspect of the growth mindset, and focus is your key to achieving new things. But how do we develop focus when our mind itself is constantly diverted? How do you even train your mind? Well, that's exactly what we are going to discuss in this chapter. Here, you will find detailed insight into the various tips you need to follow for avoiding distractions and staying focused.

Why Do You Need to Avoid Distractions?

Distractions can turn out to be a major roadblock in developing a growth mindset. When you're distracted, you no longer feel the urge or the motivation to complete your tasks. You no longer feel like reaching higher and reaching bigger. This alone is one of the biggest reasons why you need to do away with any and every kind of distraction.

How to Get Rid of Distractions?

Getting rid of distractions is easier than ever if you follow some simple guidelines. This section discusses guidelines that'll help you avoid distractions so that you're able to better focus on your tasks.

Focus Within Yourself

Before you follow any other guideline, it is really important to understand what you want from life. You can never get rid of distractions if you lack a focus in your own life. And in order to focus, you have to look within yourself. While this might sound strange, trust me, it works. All you need to do is find a quiet corner and take some time to reflect on your wants and needs. Once you have an idea about those, it's simpler and easier to tackle every big or small distraction that comes your way.

So take some time from your busy schedule and ask yourself the difficult questions. In case you have trouble concentrating, play some light music and add ambient lighting to pep up your mood. As you sit in a comfortable position, ask yourself whether you're truly satisfied with your life. Ask yourself about the things that make you happy and the things that distract you. You might not get an answer right away. But once you repeat this activity a couple of times, you'll definitely find a proper, concrete answer. This answer alone will guide you to the right path. Once you have this answer, you will get to know the things that you need to get rid of. And this is exactly how you take your very first steps in avoiding distractions.

Figure out the Cause

Once you've sorted out your most important priorities, it is time to focus on the external causes of losing focus. What exactly is bothering you while you're trying to concentrate? Does it have something to do with your office setup? Is it because of a nosy coworker? Is it because of the lack of proper skills, time, or insights for something specific that needs to be done? Is it just clear burnout? It is really important to get these answers because you'll never be able to fix the effect if you're entirely oblivious about the cause.

According to most studies, people manage to maintain their maximum focus for one to two hours a day. So it is all the more important for you to be extremely productive during this time. After you've figured out the external cause of distraction, try your best to do away with it. For instance, if your office setup bothers you, try adding a couple of motivational posters. Alternatively, if a coworker is nosy, try avoiding them or confronting them directly. Just like these two solutions, you'll find hundreds of amazing solutions for every other problem you encounter. All you have to do is give yourself the time to understand the cause.

Don't Try Too Many Things at Once

Almost all of us revel at the thought of being multi-taskers. But that's not how things work every time. And let's be really honest: if you are bogged down by twenty tasks that need to be completed every day, will you focus enough on each of them? In most cases, you won't. And I don't really blame you. None of us can expect our work to be easily completed if our focus is scattered. So instead of doing too many things at once, try focusing on only two to three things every day. Even one works just fine, but nothing should be more than your average capacity.

In case you're wondering how to start with this, the idea is pretty simple. All you need to do is to create a to-do list of your most important tasks. Remember to include the tasks that most deserve your attention on that specific day. Once you have this list ready, try filtering your options once again and check the ones that you cannot do away with for any reason. After you complete this, you'll be most possibly left with two or three tasks. So now that you have the entire day, try focusing on those tasks alone.

These are the steps that you'll need to take for accomplishing your goals with a growth mindset. As mentioned in the previous chapter, there's absolutely no harm in taking things slowly. Now that you have a to-do list, things will be much simpler.

Try Focusing on the Small Aspects of Your Work

One of the easiest ways to lose focus is by seeing your goal as the massive accomplishment it is. Since most of our goals take at least a couple of weeks or months to meet, it automatically dampens our motivation and kills our urge to do more. If you keep thinking about results, you'll either become entirely discouraged because of the nature and extent of your goal, or fantasize about what it'll seem like when you finally achieve the goal.

Both the consequences are equally detrimental for your focus, which is why you need to do away with them almost immediately. So how should you work your goal? Well, all you have to do is focus on the small chunks of work instead of the big ones. After all, which one seems simpler? Writing two hundred words every day or writing at least two sentences every day? Trying thirty push-ups every day or trying three instead?

The idea here is to work with minimums. In all probability, you'll meet them and cross them. With time, your minimum will start increasing and you will end up enhancing your ability to stay all the more focused on the bigger goals. For more help, you can also use the following techniques-

ABC Method- For this method, you'll have to divide your tasks in small chunks labeling them as A, B and C. The group A tasks are of maximum priority and have to be done right away, the group B tasks are the tasks that need to be done but have mild consequences, and the group C tasks are the tasks that can be done but don't have any consequences associated with them. Once you have this list, start with the group 'A' task and then follow it up by the group B and the group C tasks.

Pomodoro Technique- For this, you will first have to decide on the task that needs to be done and then set your Pomodoro timer for around 25 minutes. Begin with the task right after setting the timer, and as soon as the timer rings, try putting a short checkmark to check your progress. If you have lesser than four checkmarks, take a short break (for around 3-5 minutes) and then go back to set the timer for another round. After the timer rings for four times, take a longer break for around 15-30 minutes. You can then reset the timer and get back to choose another task.

Smart Sheet- In addition to these nifty techniques, there's also a tool that can help you with time management. And this is none other than Smartsheet. This is a tool that will help you in creating weekly agendas, building reports, and managing your overall appointments. The interface of this tool is pretty simple and anybody can use it.

Use Visualization Techniques

Visualization techniques go a long way in helping you stay and feel focused. But when you do visualize, you have to ensure that it's the right kind of visualization. To put it more simply, visualize yourself working. Don't visualize the success; visualize the chore.

Several champion runners have tried this technique and the results have been amazing, to say the least. These runners use the technique backwards—they imagine their success in the beginning and then go on to act out the entire process in reverse. This helps them to visualize every single step from the very beginning.

A simpler and easier way to implement this would be by imagining yourself working on a small part of your task. For instance, imagine that you're looking to play an instrument, but it's far across the room. So what should you do? Well, just try imagining yourself standing up. Once you really imagine and visualize it, acting on your visualization will be easier.

Right after that, try repeating the process of visualizing with every single step until you get your hands on the instrument and start practicing it. This entire exercise of strongly focusing on every step will distract you from negative thoughts and get your body ready for every relevant step that needs to be taken. All you have to do is apply this step every time you're struggling to focus on something. Starting with the smallest and less tedious motions will go a long way in helping you achieve your goals.

Avoid Using Your Phone for a While

If you're really looking to avoid distractions for

developing a growth mindset, start by keeping your phone off. While your phone is definitely one of the most integral aspects of proper, consistent communication, it also has the power to distract you from your current goal. When you have your phone while working, you may inadvertently get this inherent urge to check it every five to ten minutes. These five to ten minutes will eventually add up to one to two hours, thereby keeping you distracted during the prime hours of the day. When you finally put your phone down, you will no longer have the urge or dedication to work. You will feel lazy, sleepy, and incredibly distracted.

But you can't be distracted if you're looking to achieve a growth mindset. Distraction alone is your worst deterrent; it won't just kill your time but will also keep you from achieving what you want. So every time you're trying to do something important, try shutting your phone off or forward every call to voicemail. You can always check your calls once every couple of hours. I'd suggest you do the same thing with your emails. Unless it's super important, you can always check them once every couple of hours to avoid wasting unnecessary time.

Let Your Body Relax

Very often we end up getting distracted at the smallest

instance because we are too anxious to work. For me, it feels like all the muscle in my body is tense. In fact, such is the extent of the situation that I can't get myself to relax my body at any costs. If you've faced a similar situation, you might have an idea about what I'm trying to say. And guess what? One of the simplest ways to deal with this is by practicing proper muscle relaxation. You need to center this relaxation technique around your body for best results. And guess what? This won't just calm you, but it'll also help you focus better.

Is there any exercise for relaxation? How do we even start out? Well, the idea is simple. All you have to do is lie on the floor and keep your arms along the sides. As you do this, make sure you don't have your hands in fists or your feet crossed. Begin with your toes and slowly ask yourself to release them. Once you're done with this, start moving your body gently while releasing every individual body part till you reach your head. This is one of the simplest and easiest relaxation techniques that'll keep you fresh, motivated, and focused.

Get Some Fresh Air

The temperature and air circulation in your current room can end up making you feel distracted or anxious. It is very likely you'll feel fidgety if you're working in the same room for six to eight hours. This might even end up triggering a panic attack.

So if you're really looking to stay focused, start by removing yourself from the stuffy environment as soon as you can. Right after that, head outside and stay there for a while. The fresh air will help you calm down. Alternatively, the change in scenery can interrupt your distracted thought process, helping you stay focused once you're back.

If you're working for long hours, it is likely you'll get tired. But getting tired doesn't always mean you'll end up losing your focus. You can always deal with this situation by taking short breaks. So if you've been working for two to three hours at a stretch, try taking a short break of thirty to sixty minutes. Remember, your body will feel all the more refreshed if you reward it once in a while. So give it the reward it deserves by taking breaks in short, scheduled cycles.

P.S: Sometimes you also get distracted because you're hungry or dehydrated. So when you do feel the crippling sensation of hunger, don't ignore it—slow down, get some food, and you'll soon find yourself all the more focused at work.

Use Deadlines

As much as we hate deadlines, none of us can deny their relevance. When you have a specific deadline you are naturally inclined to complete the job faster than you would have if you didn't have this deadline in the first place. Deadlines can be best defined as the budget of your time. Just like budgeting money compels you to prioritize stuff, using deadlines will help you to complete the task faster. When you use them the right way, you will no longer be driven by impulse and will be able to complete your task faster.

If you get distracted easily, deadlines can be an ultimate savior as they'll compel you to focus on your work and get it done the right way.

Chapter 3: Stay Focused

Why do we emphasize staying focused? What does it have to do with being successful? Are you less stressed when you manage to be more focused? Are you happier when you have greater focus? Also, if it's really so important, why don't more people emphasize focus? If you've ever had these questions, fret not, because that is exactly what we are going to discuss in this chapter.

What Does the Term 'Focus' Mean?

While growing up, all of us stumbled upon the term 'focus.' Our parents, teachers, and elders repeatedly informed us about the importance and relevance of this single term. But what does the term even mean and how is it connected with the growth mindset? Well, being focused simply means that you have a set of clear objectives and your primary goal is to achieve those objectives. As you decide what you're planning to do, you structure your decisions on how you can achieve maximum progress towards your objectives with the limited time and resources you have at hand.

Staying focused implies that you are solely concentrating on the activity that you want to complete. Since everything else is unimportant, you shut every other door and offer your complete, undivided attention to the specific task that you're working on.

How to Achieve Focus in Your Tasks?

Well, achieving focus is easier than you'd presume. All it takes is a little practice to get the hang of things. Once you practice for a while, staying focused becomes part and parcel of your personality. But how exactly do you start out with achieving focus? Is there any specific plan that you have to follow? Luckily, there is a plan. We will discuss it in this section.

Meditate

Perhaps one of the simplest ways to achieve focus on your tasks is meditation. While it is widely used for relieving stress and relaxation, meditation also goes a long way in helping you develop a strong and consistent concentration. Now, meditation has several different techniques and none of them are wrong. In this eBook, however, I'll discuss a simple meditation technique that is ideal for people who are starting out. My technique deals with meditation and positive affirmation, both of which collectively help you in strengthening your focus.

The idea of this meditative exercise is simple. All you need to do is find a quiet spot in your room or anywhere else you deem fit. Once you find this spot, light some scented candles and sit comfortably in a corner. Now, close your eyes and try to get rid of all your disturbing and distracting thoughts. I know, this is easier said than done. But try it for a while. In case you can't seem to remove your thoughts, try playing light music in the background. Now, as you close your eyes and reach a clear state of mind, try focusing on the things that deserve your attention. This can be a pending assignment, your upcoming exam, or anything of equal (or greater) importance.

As you start thinking about this task, start visualizing yourself doing it. Now repeat a positive, motivating affirmation that'll inspire you to do the task. You can say something along the lines of "I need to complete this assignment by April 8 and I will do it" or "I will focus on my current assignment and won't be distracted by Facebook." Regardless of the affirmation you use, make it a point to repeat it. This will not just boost your motivation but will also push you to move ahead of your boundaries. Once you practice meditation and keep doing it once in a while, you will soon get the hang of it and manage to focus on your tasks better.

Train Your Brain

As bizarre as it sounds, you can actually train your brain with the right technique. Since your brain is nothing but mental muscle, it can always be trained if you teach it the right things. But what are these 'right things'? Well, these are nothing but exercises. Platforms like Cogmed and Lumosity have brain-training exercises. Download these applications and follow the exercises for best results.

If, however, you're not really comfortable using an app, there's yet another simple way. For this, all you need to do is communicate with your subconscious. Start out by creating a routine, where you repeat certain things before going to sleep. For instance, you want your mind to focus on the important task that you need to complete the following day. In this case, sit quietly, and right before you sleep, tell your brain that you need the task to be done with complete focus.

Inform it of the reasons why you cannot afford to miss it any case. Tell your brain about the positive impact this task will have on your life. After doing this, get a few hours of uninterrupted sleep. You should ideally sleep for seven hours for this exercise to work the right way. And guess what? Once you wake up and try focusing on the task, you'll be miraculously able to complete it. Your subconscious is a living entity just like you. So if you manage to communicate the right things, it'll surely work in your favor.

Designate Specific Hours for Specific Tasks

Yet another simple and effective way to focus better is by designating specific hours for specific tasks. For instance, if you have a project that requires plenty of calculation and another one that requires you to sift through emails, you should schedule the project involving calculations in the morning as your brain will most likely be extremely productive at this hour. Since you'll just be waking up from sleep, you won't be tired nor distracted. You can give your full attention to the project and complete it successfully.

Alternatively, when you keep the email checking business for the wee hours of the night, you'll be able to do it better. Since it doesn't require much mental work, it'll hardly take you a couple of minutes to go through the entire thing. So this is exactly what you need to do. You have to strategize, plan, manage, and program things so that everything works according to your convenience. While I do know that there are days when nothing goes to plan, there's still no harm in planning stuff. Once you have a blueprint of your day, focusing and doing things gets easier and a tad more hassle-free.

Follow the Right Diet

While many people discredit the role of diet in focusing better, such is not always the case. The right diet doesn't just help you stay healthy; it also goes a long way in helping you develop a solid growth mindset. Packaged stuff, takeaway meals, and stuff with excessive sugar doesn't just have a detrimental impact on your body but it also hampers your productivity and overall ability to focus.

This is exactly why you need to introduce healthy food habits into your regular routine. For instance, you can swap packaged meals for healthy veggies and whip them up in a delicious salad. Or you can replace your fried chicken with grilled chicken drumsticks that come with a healthy veggie dipping. Nowadays, you'll find hundreds of food videos online that'll motivate you to cook. So whip up your meals and follow a healthy diet for better focus and improved concentration.

P.S: Grab a small cup of coffee if you're feeling slightly groggy. While caffeine is bad, it can definitely improve your focus when taken in moderation. So if you're fatigued after a long day, and still have some important task to cover, this is a foolproof way to enhance your concentration.

Try Being Mindful

In addition to meditation, try practicing mindfulness throughout the entire day. For the uninitiated, mindfulness is the act of focusing on your present, slowing down a bit and gently observing the physical (and) emotional experiences that you encounter at the current moment.

One of the best ways to practice mindfulness is at mealtime. Try taking a little bit more time to chew your meals. Try concentrating on the flavors and texture of the meal. Alternatively, you can also try this while you're shaving. During this time, you will inhale the powerful fragrance of your shaving cream. Experience this fragrance and let it linger. Right after that, enjoy the pleasure of adding warm lather to your face. Do this by gently dragging your razor along the stubble.

Allocating short sessions for mindfulness during the entire day won't just keep you happier, but it'll also strengthen your attention span during the time you actually need it. Mindfulness, if practiced properly, can also help you in pushing back every single distraction that comes your way.

So, if you're working on a specific task and get this restless urge to try something else, remind yourself about the importance of being in the present. Repeat the affirmation "I need to be in the present moment" for best results. It is within this moment that your body will be aware and your mind will follow suit. Try focusing on your breath for a while. After a couple of seconds, you'll realize that you no longer have any distractions and are comfortable to start work once again.

Be Curious

The more curious you manage to be, the greater the power of your focus is going to be, every time you take on a new endeavor. Since we already discussed the role of curiosity in the previous chapters, you now have a basic idea about it. It is this relentless thirst for knowledge that'll help you develop and achieve growth mindset.

Prioritize Your Workload

Very often when your work starts piling up, it might seem like you'd never be able to catch up. In times like these, it becomes incredibly difficult to figure out where exactly you need to start, and this alone leads you to waste your valuable time. In order to avoid this situation, you can always prioritize your workload.

You can start out by making a to-do list for the things you need to do throughout the day. Once you have this list ready, start filtering the options by labeling them as 'Very important,' 'important' and 'moderately important.' Once you have this list ready, you automatically know which task deserves your maximum time and which one can be dealt with later. For instance, if you have to complete your pending assignment and visit your dentist on the same day, you'd know which one needs to be dealt with faster. Structuring workloads and setting realistic deadlines goes a long way in helping you complete your job faster.

Chapter 4: Practicing Good Habits

Since we humans are products of habit, cultivating them should be easy, right? Well, that's not how it works in every case.

The problem is that we end up getting comfortable doing certain things in a specific way, every single day. So before we realize it, we end up inadvertently following a specific routine without weighing its effectiveness or feasibility.

Sadly, not every habit that we cultivate can be deemed good. For instance, if we have the habit of drinking a glass of alcohol, every time we head home after work, it'll end up having a detrimental impact on our health. Similarly, if we tend to snack on unhealthy junk while binging on our favorite TV series, that, too, can adversely impact our health. And these are just two minor instances of habits impacting us adversely. If you think about it, you'll find hundreds of such instances where we purposely or inadvertently cultivate certain habits that affect our growth mindset and keep us from achieving what we want in life. Since a growth mindset is strongly interlinked with our habits, in this chapter you will find detailed insights on practicing and cultivating good habits.

Why Is It Important to Develop Good Habits?

Developing good habits goes hand in hand with helping you achieve a growth mindset. At this point you already know about the basic philosophy of growth mindset, so grasping this should be easier. Since the growth mindset deals with having the flexibility to achieve bigger and better goals, habits play a significant role in its development. After all, it is only when you develop the habit to be flexible and create newer goals that you will be truly able to achieve this mindset. The right set of habits won't just positively transform you, but they will also go a long way in making you a better and more sensitive person.

How to Develop Good Habits?

Now that you know everything about good habits, you might be wondering how to develop them in the first place. In this section you will find an answer to every query you have about developing new, good habits. So whether you're just starting out, or someone who's in the middle of a rut, here are some guidelines that'll definitely help you.

Choose Your Activities Mindfully

In the previous chapter, we discussed the importance of being mindful. So now that you have a basic idea about it, start off by choosing your habits mindfully. Since your habit alone is going to have a long-term impact on your lifestyle, try choosing an activity that resonates with your goal and reflects on the kind of person you are.

If you don't choose this activity, you'll find yourself doing the same things that you usually do. Since some of these factors are too ingrained to be changed, your new habit won't really take a root. So if you're choosing a new practice, try considering a couple of factors like your inherent strengths, your abilities, your lifestyle, and the overall complexity of the habit you've chosen. Alternatively, you should also check with your current level of stress and the time you have available so that you finally develop a habit that perfectly teams up with these different variables.

If you're still unsure about the variables, try taking online personality tests or using apps to understand the kind of personality you have. There are plenty of options to help you in this regard. And the best part is that these online tools won't just assess the stress relievers that work best with your lifestyle, but they also offer you a list of things that you can try right away.

Make the Right Decision and Be Committed in Your Goal

I know, saying this is easier than working for it. But trust me, once you get the hang of it, nothing will seem simpler. After you've taken your personality test and figured out more about the unknown facets, try making the right decision. Make a decision that fits and works with your lifestyle. Since you're trying to achieve a growth mindset, you're not in a competition with anybody. You are in a complete position to make your decision for yourself.

But despite weighing the benefits, many of us choose to procrastinate. Remember, procrastinating isn't a solution here, and procrastination can never be a solution if you're planning to achieve a growth mindset. Since this mindset draws heavily on escaping your comfort zone, you first have to do away with procrastination even before trying to develop the habit. Once you do this, try being positive about the impact this habit will have in your life. In case you're not too confident about yourself, try setting small reminders that'll remind you about the decision pertaining to the habit you're yet to make.

Finally, when you do make the decision, try sticking to your goal. Sticking to your habit is even more important than choosing the habit in the first place. Can't we all choose a habit? We can. So the important part here is to stick to this habit and follow at all costs. Once you're serious about the habit, achieving it will be easier than ever. Studies suggest you develop new habits after doing a task consistently for fourteen days. So keep doing it, till it becomes deeply wired in your brain—and when it actually does, try living up to it.

Get Support

You'll be more successful with your habits if you find a couple of people who are willing to stand by you. These individuals won't just give you the kind of support you need, but they will also be the people who you look up to. When you list a group of close people for this job, you will automatically be answerable to them. So if you feel like ditching your habit for something else, they can reprimand you and guide you back to the right path.

One of the best ways to get support for your cause is by hiring a personal coach. In fact, you'll find plenty of such coaches in leading online websites. Alternatively, you can also get this support by getting someone to start the habit with you. So if you're planning to join the gym, try getting a gym buddy; or if you're planning to write at least one page a day, find someone who's willing to try it with you. Trust me, this is way better than doing something alone and sulking about it throughout the day.

If, however, you have no other option and plan on doing this alone, ask a friend or a close confidant who'll help you be accountable for the first couple of weeks. You can also try using a journal in order to record your daily activities, successes, and failures every single day or by the end of a single week. Regardless of the route you've chosen, it is always better to have someone by your side, at least when you're just starting out.

Identify the Roadblocks and Triggers

If you aren't sure about your triggers, or are entirely underprepared for the impending roadblocks, you will end up failing to achieve your habits. So even before you develop a new habit, find out about the habits that currently define you. Almost every one of us have several moments of vulnerability or weakness where we need consistent support to release and vent our frustrations.

Resorting to alcohol, drugs, binge eating, or medication

won't help you here. So if an unpleasant roadblock hinders your performance at work, or if you find yourself in the middle of a messy traffic jam while returning home, try finding a healthy and better alternative to your conventional way of handling it.

All of us have our fair share of bad days. But having bad days doesn't mean we have to resort to unhealthy habits for alleviating stress. At the same time, we cannot let our boredom, grief, or anger act as a trigger for our bad habits. So, even before you start out with your new habit, try finding some healthy ways that can be used for dealing with these roadblocks and triggers. This will help you stay focused and you'll also end up achieving your goal sooner than you had presumed.

Use Rewards

Although the very feeling of sticking to habit alone is an excellent reward, it is also equally important to get your fair share of tangible rewards. For instance, think about the times when your teachers used stars and other tokens of appreciation to encourage your good behavior; or how you trained your pets with a couple of small treats. And guess what? No matter how much we deny it, all of us are fond of rewards.

The idea here is to reward yourself for the first couple of steps, until this new habit becomes a part and parcel of your personality. This is all the more viable for the first month, since this is the approximate time it'll take for a random behavior to change into a habit.

The rewards you choose to give yourself are entirely your personal choice as you know the best incentive for your little successes. Having said that, it's advisable to give yourself something small and truly enjoyable. *Small* is particularly important because big stuff can distract you from your goal.

I'll give you a small example here. When I started hitting the gym, in the beginning, I'd reward every fifth visit to the gym with a new workout T-shirt. That way I'd get the feeling I'd earned the new outfit. At the same time, I'd also find myself looking better every time I headed to the dressing room. A couple of my other friends chose to give themselves a piece of chocolate, pedometers, good music, and pretty little pens. You can either take these ideas or come up with something new to boost your habit and make it a part of your life.

Track Your Progress

As you move ahead in developing healthy habits, it is also important to pay special attention to the way you feel when you incorporate these habits into your life. Does your current practice seem to sync with your personality and lifestyle? Can you maintain your new habits comfortably, or do you need added support? If you realize that you haven't managed to keep up with the plans you made, don't sweat it! Instead of berating yourself and switching to self-loathing mode, try congratulating yourself for observing a significant change in your plans. This alone is extremely important since it's one of the very first steps in building a solid plan.

Alternatively, if you're really struggling to keep up the habit, and have figured out that you need to try an entirely different thing, then you have an idea about what doesn't work for you. In this way, you also get to try something different that you might eventually fall in love with. In either case, it is always better to learn these new things about yourself as they go a long way in helping you evolve as an individual.

Remember, the coolest part of developing these new habits is that once you do them repeatedly, they automatically become a part of your lifestyle. In fact, anything you've been doing for long enough eventually turns out to be a habit. And right after it does, you'll no longer have to put added effort into it. Such is the joy and charm of developing these good habits. So if you're struggling to start with a new habit and are wondering how to make things work your way, this guideline will surely work in your favor.

Chapter 5: Appreciate Your Manifestation Power

If you've been using social media of late, 'manifest' is something that you've probably heard of. But how big is this buzzword, and what does it have to do with your success? Well, that is exactly what we will discuss in this chapter. Here, you will find detailed insight on everything you wanted to know about your manifestation power. Additionally, you will also get to know the ways in which this power can be used and implemented to its maximum potential.

What Is the Power of Manifestation All About?

In the simplest terms, the power of manifestation is our inherent ability to create the kind of world we have around us. This thought alone is powerful, isn't it? According to the law of manifestation, we are entirely responsible for the kind of world and reality we have around ourselves. At times, it might seem absolutely impossible to believe this, particularly when nothing is going right. But trust me, when implemented the right way, manifestation power can truly transform the life and world around you.

However, for the power of manifestation to work the right way, you have to ensure a proper ethical and moral framework. In other words, if you're looking to manifest power to enhance your growth mindset, you'll need to have a solid purpose behind using it in the first place. This purpose should serve you and work in your favor. It should provide you satisfaction and make a difference to the world around you.

How Is Gratitude Relevant for Implementing Your Manifesting Power?

When you are thankful and appreciative of the kind of person you are right now, you immediately and inadvertently raise your 'feel-good' vibes, which further exudes greater vibrational energy. And in return? You'll remain in a constant state of alignment with the world around you. In other words, your manifestation process will turn around quickly and more easily.

When you sit back and dwell on the things you don't yet have, you end up being impatient and almost immediately, you'll find yourself wanting something else.

Remember, you can only achieve instant manifestation if you are thankful for the kind of life you have. Also, gratitude shouldn't just be a part of your manifestation process but a significant aspect of your overall well-being. But how exactly do you appreciate your manifestation power and implement it to its full potential? Well, to start with, you have to be open-minded.

Every day you'll come across people who have wonderful lives and others who could enjoy a better state of being. But have you noticed one thing? Most of the people who need better lives have one specific thing in common—they are not grateful for the kind of things they already have. And that is exactly where they are going wrong. Remember, you can never gain more until you are appreciative of the things you have already gained. This lack of gratitude will close you off from achieving more and will eventually bog you down.

No matter how difficult your life is, you can always find something to be grateful about. And guess what? As soon as you find this aspect, your life will drastically improve.

The act of complaining is nothing but focusing on the

aspects that your mind deems to be an issue. The universe is aware of the fact that there aren't any big problems to deter you from your goal. In fact, everything was made by you, and you alone have the power to change the things around you. Whether this is for better or worse is completely in your control.

If you're looking to lose the amazing things you have in your life, if you want to experience difficult days, if you want to be in a rut every time you have to pay your bills, or if you really want to feel unappreciated in a relationship, all you need to do is *complain*.

Alternatively, if you want your life to be better in practically every way, if you want to achieve more wealth, if you're looking to experience happy, beautiful relationships, if you want to be inherently satisfied, you need to be grateful.

In case you don't know already, it is gratitude, and gratitude alone, that has the power to create abundance. Contrarily, it is complaining that brings forth poverty.

So don't brood about the things that are 'wrong' in your life. This vision of how you're presuming your life to be has the power to change it. So visualize the kind of life where you want to exist and you'll soon find it expanding in every single area. You'll feel happy and joyful as things quickly move in your favor, thereby making it all the more magnificent and magical.

Since you're already connected to the creative energy of the world around you, no matter how difficult your life seems right now, you alone have the power of making it enjoyable and better. As you now have an idea about this transformative ability, start being grateful and appreciative about the things around you and the things that are likely to happen.

If you truly want to transform your life; if you truly want to enhance the power of manifestation, if you truly want to achieve the growth mindset; start being grateful, starting today. Gratitude alone is a quick, simple, and effective energy that has the power to produce amazing results.

If you try thinking about the number of things that you should be grateful for at this moment, you'll be amazed to find innumerable things at your disposal. Be grateful for the littlest of things around you, as they, too, have the ability to truly transform your life for good.

Having said that, being grateful and appreciative despite the trials and tribulations of life can be difficult. And that is exactly why we've developed the following guidelines that'll help you practice being appreciative of your manifesting power.

Swap 'I Have to' for 'I Get to'

Every time you get up from your bed in the morning, what are your very first thoughts? Maybe they're something along the lines of "I need to do this" or "I have to complete that assignment." While there's nothing inherently wrong with that statement, every time you say "I have to" or "I need to," you end up feeling like your life is entirely on your shoulders, and you can't find enough time to appreciate it. Although this is a common attitude, it doesn't mean it is the right kind of attitude.

A better way to deal with this would be by swapping your "I need to" for "I'm getting a chance to." This will not only compel you to think twice about your privilege, but will also shed light on the various aspects of life that you've been taking for granted. So all you need to do is implement this simple and effective way of expressing your gratitude on a daily basis.

One of the biggest changes that you can make right now is to tell yourself that you are getting a chance to do the things that you're doing. You're not merely doing them because you have to do them, but because you're getting this beautiful chance that everyone doesn't get to have. As you do this, you will notice a subtle change in your appreciation for the things you have. Remember, the current aspects of your life might not be someone else's reality. So try to be appreciative of the kind of privilege you have right now.

This simple perspective can transform your entire perspective about life alone! And the best part is that it'll speed your possibilities of instant manifestation which will eventually help you achieve a growth mindset.

Be Grateful for the Smallest of Things

Another way in which you can consciously appreciate your manifesting power is by being grateful for the smallest of things. Even if nothing happens throughout the day, be thankful for the new day and the new opportunity that tags along with it.

Every day, we wake up and do our chores, taking these very activities for granted. Don't believe me? Okay, so when did you last appreciate the fact that you're alive? In all probability, you didn't, and that is exactly what you need to change.

So every time you wake up, be thankful for the precious gift of life. Additionally, also try being grateful for the simplest of things that happen throughout the day. For instance, if you're driving and suddenly approach a green light, be thankful for that. Every time you find an empty parking space, be grateful and express that gratitude. The more grateful you are throughout the day, the better your day will get.

By expressing your gratitude, you're telling the universe that you've been truly grateful for the ways in which it has served you. And that's not all! You'll also end up feeling happier and more content with your current life by following this simple exercise. Remember, the act of being grateful doesn't imply that you have to disregard your current desires. It simply means that you're exuding the right vibrations. These vibrations will eventually help you implement your manifesting power, thereby letting you achieve everything that you want to do.

Working on the Power of Manifestation

While being appreciative is extremely important in order

to ensure that your power of manifestation works, there's also something else that you have to do. In case you haven't guessed already, I'm suggesting you follow and do something that excites you to the core.

For this, you first need to be clear about the things in life that excite you to the core and the things that don't have that much of an impact in your life. Following this highest level of excitement will fuel you with the necessary creative energy. So next time you're high on excitement, your energy and your manifestation power will be high at the same time.

Make a list of the things that truly give you joy in life. These should be the kind of activities where you don't even have to keep track of time. Right after that, try filling your days with these activities as much as you can. Every time you're in harmony with the kind of things you love, you'll end up receiving them in abundance.

Another equally useful way to use your manifestation power is by setting your intentions. Be really honest with yourself and try to be clear about the intentions you have. Your intentions are the creative force behind every manifestation you work on. It is these intentions that'll imbue a sense of vibration in you that'll compel the universe to draw forth everything that you're looking to achieve in life. You can either journal these intentions, speak about them, or come up with a vision board. The important aspect here is to feel that things are happening for you, and working in your favor. Right after this, relinquish this sense of attachment and the universe will work its charm in helping you use your manifestation power to its maximum potential.

Finally, once you're done with everything else, try clearing some space. Even before you begin the process of manifestation, it is important to take some time in releasing any disbelief that stands as a hurdle before your happiness. One of the best ways to achieve this is by praying for release. Start with a daily prayer where you ask the universe to remove the shackles of limiting insights as these very insights stand in the way of your inherent beliefs.

You need to be open for the signs you get from the universe. Alternatively, you also need to be present for the assignments that have been brought entirely for you. These universal assignments might come in several forms. All you need to do is identify them to work your way around.

Once you follow these guidelines, achieving a growth mindset with your power of manifestation will be easier than ever.

Mindset for Success

Chapter 6: Increase and Reinforce Your Knowledge

As we've mentioned in the previous chapters, your brain requires exercise just like any other muscle. And perhaps one of the simplest ways to ensure this exercise is by increasing and reinforcing your knowledge base. Increasing knowledge stands as one of the primary facets of the growth mindset itself. So when you actually take corrective measures to work on this aspect, you inadvertently take a step forward towards a growth mindset. In this chapter, we will discuss in detail the exercises you can try in order to reinforce your knowledge. You will also find insight into the relationship between knowledge and the growth mindset.

How Is Increasing Knowledge Linked with the Growth Mindset?

At this point, you already know that a growth mindset deals with a continuous process of learning. It doesn't have any place for fixed learning goals. This alone perfectly defines the relationship between the growth mindset and your knowledge base. When you compel yourself to move forward and set new goals in terms of learning, you automatically take a step further in achieving a growth mindset. Since this mindset itself deals with learning new stuff with each passing day, reinforcing knowledge is an integral part of it. It is only when you relentlessly pursue knowledge that you're able to understand and perceive this mindset better.

How to Increase and Reinforce My Knowledge

Reinforcing knowledge is a continuous process. It can never happen overnight. The entire act takes plenty of effort, consistency, and dedication. After all, it is only when you're dedicated that you have the burning desire to know more. But how exactly does one start with reinforcing their knowledge? Are there any specific guidelines to follow? Luckily, there is a guideline, and it is discussed in the following section.

Don't Stop Reading

You might have completed your school, university, or any other institution where you were required to read. However, that doesn't in any way signify that you don't have to read anymore. Just like the growth mindset itself, reading is a continuous process. This is possibly the reason why successful people advocate for reading every day.

Reading won't just expand your knowledge, but it'll also keep your brain active. By reading, you are taking part in an activity that requires you to constantly process information. And this alone plays a vital role in helping you conceptualize new ideas and insights. As you read more, you learn about various different subjects from different perspectives. This understanding of perspectives goes a long way in making you flexible and open to knowledge.

If you're a creative individual, reading is even more essential for you. Whether you're looking for some solid inspiration for your upcoming art project or are simply sifting through topics for your next novel, all you need to do is read. Whether it's a novel, a piece of poetry, a nonfiction essay, or anything else, the right words will inadvertently get wired in your brain and compel you to push your boundaries.

In case you're still skeptical about reading in this digital age, just remember one thing: every answer to your question is written amid the lines of your favorite literary pieces. In case you're on a budget and can't afford a new book, go for the second-hand ones or the digital copies. Alternatively, you can also head to your local library. Your library holds numerous possibilities for learning new stuff. So when you head there, you actually end up taking an actual, concrete initiative in achieving a growth mindset.

P.S: If you're not really fond of reading and are wondering how to do it, let a friend tag along with you. When you try your new reading sessions with a close buddy, everything gets better and more enjoyable.

Take up an Online Course

Many individuals have a very fixed notion about learning. For them, learning is only possible in the confined rooms of a school, university, or similar institution. But guess what? That needn't be the case. Our age is the age of digitalization, where anything can happen at anytime. While this does have its fair share of dangers, the advantages are amazing. And one of the biggest advantages is the availability of online courses.

Right now, you'll find hundreds of platforms that offer online courses on a wide range of subjects. So all you need to do is choose your subject and start learning right away. Trust me; it doesn't matter if you're a student or a professional. And the best part is that you'll find plenty of subjects that are not just fun to study about, but are also equally interesting. So if you dreaded learning in college and missed out on opportunities, here's a new chance to start afresh.

I've personally used platforms like Coursera and Skillshare and my experience has been amazing. You'll find many other similar platforms where you can learn about anything under the sun. All you need is to have the enthusiasm and the motivation to learn.

Most of these online platforms come with short courses that are further classified in smaller sections. This means you won't have to go through the entire class in a single setting. The teachers are experienced professionals in their respective fields, so you can always count on them for guidelines on your upcoming projects. Additionally, you can share your work with the entire class and get their valuable feedback.

When you join these platforms, you'll notice that, at times, the classes can be as massive as 5000 people.

However, they can be as small as 100 people. And this is the beauty of this technology. Unlike conventional classes, these online courses do not come with specific deadlines. Here, you get to work at your preferred pace, so you can come up with something truly amazing.

Quite recently I took up a course on soapmaking and interior design. The entire activity made me excited like a kid. I was engaged, hooked, and my creative potential was at its fullest.

In case you're still not confident about the online courses, you can always try in-person courses and workshops. They are incredible, insightful, and equally interactive. But there's a small downside. Unlike the online courses, these can be pretty pricey. So if you're just starting out with enhancing your knowledge base, I'd suggest you go ahead with the online courses.

Remember, there's an entirely new world that is waiting for you to be explored. So all you need to do is get started and choose your field. Once you make your choice, every other thing will fall into place.

Watch Plenty of Documentaries

As boring as it sounds, documentaries are yet another excellent way to reinforce your knowledge. This is all the more ideal for people who aren't really fond of reading. There are hundreds of digital platforms with insightful documentaries about any and every topic under the sun. All you need to do is explore them and take your pick. And if you do end up finding something to watch, it'll surely turn out to be one of your most exciting hours watching TV!

In case you don't really frequent digital platforms, TV channels like National Geographic, Discovery TV, or the History Channel can make the cut. Each of these channels comes with interesting documentaries about humans, animals, food, plants, fish, dinosaurs, and what not!

For others, there's Netflix and YouTube. In case you're not really sure about the kind of things you're looking to watch, try using public forums like IMDB, Rotten Tomatoes, or Reddit. When you ask a question about the best documentaries to watch, you'll be inundated with suggestions from these platforms. And who knows? You might even end up making some good friends.

Documentaries are an excellent way to stay engaged

while learning something new. Use them to their maximum potential to get your daily dose of insight while remaining comfortably seated on your couch!

Travel to New Destinations

Yes, you read that right—traveling has a positive impact on your career and learning potential. The idea behind this is pretty simple. When you leave your comfort zone in order to travel, you end up getting much-needed motivation and exposure which is imperative to performing better in your workplace and to learning something new. Traveling kickstarts your creativity and helps you come up with ideas that you would never consider if you kept following your same, boring routine. Your newfound traveling experiences will collectively help you to figure out new ways of dealing with your old problems. In certain cases it might also open ways for new business contracts or some new career path that you were initially unaware of.

In addition to this, traveling also makes you more confident and helps you hone your communication skills. When you explore a place you haven't visited before, it automatically builds your confidence which eventually has a positive impact on your career. Also, since you're communicating with many new people of diverse cultures and race, your communication skills will significantly improve. Even if you don't learn a new language, you'll be able to communicate with your colleagues better. To put it simply, traveling will prepare you for the 'real life' that awaits you. It'll train you, guide you, and help you perform better in almost every facet and phase of your life.

Don't Be Afraid of Asking New Questions

This is probably one of the most important things that have a significant impact on learning and the reinforcement of knowledge. In order to develop a growth mindset, you need to have a relentless quest for knowledge. And this is perhaps best manifested when you start asking more and more questions.

Every time you meet someone new, try asking them questions. Ask everyone about everything happening in their lives. This won't make you annoying or nosy. It'll just open your perspective to a newer world and newer ideas. As people about the kind of jobs they do and whether or not they are satisfied with it; ask them about their favorite hobbies and the things that amuse them. While there are always a couple of introverts, you'll also find others who enjoy talking about themselves. They'll tell you their stories of their successes, failures, and what not. And let's be honest—is there a better way to learn, if not from stories?

You'd be amazed by the number of things you can learn from your best friend at work. All you have to do is ask the right things. You have to ask things that'll strike a chord, make them comfortable, and compel them to speak more often.

Remember, learning doesn't necessarily have to be a burden. It can be incredibly exciting, if you manage to do the right things. It can be rife with new things and amazing ideas. All you have to do is take a step out of your comfort zone. And don't be afraid to learn new things. Just think about all the things that you can manage to learn within the following month!

So what's stopping you? What's keeping you back? Leave your worries at home, and try stepping into a new world of knowledge. Once you take this first step, things will automatically get easier. You just have to be brave enough to take the step and make the move.

Chapter 7: Stimulate Your Creative, Intuitive Mind

The smart inventor, the innovative entrepreneur, the ingenious scientist, or the avid writer— regardless of your field or domain, all of us want to be more creative. All of us seek the creative genius that'll not just transform our work, but also open doors for new possibilities. All of us seek the original, transformative genius that has the ability to transform the world around us. In this chapter, we'll discuss the various ways in which you can stimulate your creative, intuitive mind.

Why Do You Need to Stimulate Your Creative Mind?

Most of us deem creativity to be an awe-inducing, magical gift that people inherently possess. But just like we can express creativity in various different ways, you can also learn and hone it like every other skill. Fostering your creativity is imperative to the development of a growth mindset as it helps you evolve as an individual. Also, since the modern world doesn't have any room for the mundane and boring, it is extremely important to cultivate your creativity and utilize it to the maximum potential. In the next section, we discuss various ways in which you can stimulate your creative spirit.

Use Both Sides of Your Brain

There's a common myth that suggests right-brained people are relatively more creative than the left-brained ones. Contrary to the right-brained individuals, these left-brained people are deemed to be more analytical and thoughtful. But guess what? This is nothing but an absolutely baseless myth. You can only achieve true creativity by using both the sides of your mind, or more specifically, both sides of your entire brain. So there's absolutely no point in leaving one side out, just for the sake of baseless assumptions.

Your most imaginative insights will be both logical and rational. Alternatively, your scientific and analytical approaches will be unique and out of the box. In order to succeed in life and achieve a growth mindset, you will have to collectively work with all the mentioned aspects. So there's no way you can leave one out, just because you think it came from the right or left brain.

This entire idea of right- and left-brained theory comes from Roger Sperry's split-brain hypothesis. His research dates back to the early 1960s, and according to it, certain activities of your brain, like spatial reasoning, are stimulated by the right hemisphere of your brain. Contrarily, aspects like language and analytical thoughts are stimulated by your brain's left hemisphere. He was the first person to research this, and following his research, there weren't any other substantial studies on this topic.

And this is exactly why you need to leave this myth aside and follow a whole-brain approach in your tasks. Remember, it is only a whole-brained approach that requires additional thinking/lateral thinking that compels you to consider various different perspectives. When you manage to think outside the box, you'll also end up devising fresh approaches to solving different problems and conquering tough challenges.

Due to this, you should work to ensure that your whole brain is used, instead of just a specific side. You can try this by doing unique stuff and following it up with absolutely contradictory stuff. For instance, do some origami and immediately follow it up with an uninterrupted session of logical reasoning and mathematics. You can also try other unconventional stuff like writing something with your left hand (or right hand if the left is your dominant hand).

You will only enjoy creative prowess when you manage to perceive things differently. For instance, you can wear your watch on the opposite wrist, use your phone upside down, or even write something backwards. As bizarre as it sounds, it did work for a couple of people, namely Leonardo Da Vinci, who ended up discovering mirror writing.

So all you have to do is be out of the box, and come up with something unique. Do not let anything deter you from your goal. Remember, it is the very act of escaping your comfort zone that'll eventually train and hone you.

Always Have the Desire to Learn More

This is yet another habit that won't just boost your creativity, but will also help you move a step forward in achieving a growth mindset. If your mind is thoughtful and your thoughts are intelligent, you'll experience a constant urge to know and learn more. And this is exactly what you need in order to develop a growth mindset. It is your lifelong thirst for knowledge that'll truly fuel your creativity. And when you are d creative, your thoughts are bound to expand.

By taking part in a continuous process of learning, you

inadvertently give your mind the much- needed ideas that help you to think better. People become broadminded by cultivating this very habit. They become broadminded as they are open to novel concepts and unique approaches. So if you have the same goal, it's high time to start.

In order to achieve a growth mindset through creativity, you need to be willing to try unique ideas. You can't achieve this mindset if you end up dismissing everything that is beyond your comfort zone. In order to be successful, you have to be open to new ideas and thoughts. So even if you disagree with something/someone, you have to give them a chance to express their opinion.

Communication can never be a one-way street. In order to communicate, you have to be willing and curious enough to express your concerns about the things happening around you. You need to question more often. Most importantly, you need to be motivated to learn more about the world where you live.

If you're just starting out with this, I'd suggest you work on your vertical knowledge in the beginning. This vertical knowledge is your urge to dive deep in a specific topic. Additionally, I'd also recommend you work on your horizontal knowledge. This horizontal knowledge is your understanding and insights about various different fields.

Having the necessary knowledge in different areas of your life will offer you the backdrop for new ideas. At the same time, familiarity with a specific area will give you the necessary insight to work towards innovation in that specific field.

Face Challenges

You can never be successful if you're too apprehensive or anxious about challenges. This is primarily because challenges are one of the most significant aspects of any worthwhile project. If you're looking to be successful by cultivating your growth mindset, you need to have the strength to accept new challenges.

Remember, it is only during these challenges when you will develop a solid depth of character. When you meet your challenges without thinking twice, you unknowingly build your resilience in facing bigger challenges that you might encounter in the long run. Confronting these challenges will reduce your ego and give you the humility to realize that there are certain things in life that have to be learned from. It'll make you realize that there's nothing wrong with making mistakes.

When you take proper action while facing a challenge,

you also develop a sense of personal responsibility. This is because you cannot seek help from others, nor can you blame them. This confidence and pride from achieving a difficult task will free your mind and compel your spirit to be more kind, understanding, and generous. Additionally, it'll also improve your thoughtfulness. You can only achieve success when you let compassion rule and open doors for new ideas.

Explain Things to Yourself

When you're creative, you're also required to process and understand the details that you've been furnished with. After all, it's one thing to watch a documentary or flip through the pages of a book and an entirely different thing to be confident enough to explain the same topic to somebody else. When you're able to express and explain this new insight, it automatically indicates that you've processed this information on a greater level.

As you explain something to yourself, you also get a chance to expand it, mold it, and furnish it with your own vision. This idea that you came across is now integrated with your inherent perspectives and ideas. You can also follow several threads of ideas for creating newer concepts.

However, even before you start, remember one thing. In order to be a good explainer, you're also required to be someone who listens well. In fact, can you ever properly absorb and retain details about something that you didn't even hear properly in the first place?

So if you're really looking to hone your creative abilities, I'd suggest you develop this habit of explaining things to yourself. This will play a vital role in helping you solidify the knowledge you gain. It'll also help you in thinking through areas that require improvement. This exercise will further strengthen your ability to brainstorm and build new concepts.

Turn on Your Creative Side

Have you ever been really focused on some important task, feeling like you've been performing exceptionally well, only to eventually realize that the ideas you've used are boring and redundant?

According to a study published by the *Harvard Business Review*, we have a natural inclination to continue working on a specific task even when we're nowhere close to the desired results. Also, while working on some project that involves creativity, we end up reaching a dead end without even realizing it. So how do we avoid this situation and prevent it from being a hindrance to our final goals?

Well, the idea is simple—all you have to do is take proper, consistent breaks at regular intervals. This will give your mind an opportunity to be refreshed. If you're just starting out with this activity, try using a timer and start switching tasks almost immediately after it goes off.

At this point, you can do something else, get some fresh air outside, and then go back to your original job. As you do this, it'll help you to be creative while also keeping your ideas fresh and out of the box.

If at any point you find yourself having trouble in completing a goal, try looking at your problem from an entirely different perspective. This will help you approach your task in an unconventional way. You might start working backwards or work the problem from a different angle. Taking breaks is imperative to foster creativity as they compel you to think differently and work on your goals with a unique perspective.

Be Imaginative

It goes without saying that, in order to be creative, you have to let your imagination run wild. Perhaps one of the simplest ways to do this is by tapping into the inherent imaginativeness you possessed as a little kid. Think about the times when you enjoyed playing pretend. It was at this point when you mastered the art of creating entirely arbitrary worlds where anything and everything was possible. You enjoyed this bit and loved challenging yourself with new games and tests.

Give yourself some time, and give your mind the chance to wander; it needs this. Once you've imagined, use the ideas as part of a brainstorming session. Try challenging yourself with the most creative exercises. This can be anything from doodling in your sketchbook to writing a piece of flash fiction.

Try keeping a full journal of the ideas you've come up with; it doesn't matter if they are impractical or bizarre. Giving your mind the opportunity to dream is one of the most crucial aspects of the problem-solving process in general. Alternatively, it is also one of the best ways to strengthen your creative muscles. Once you cultivate an imaginative mind that's open to every possibility, your innate creative genius will start flourishing and working in your favor. And the best part is that you'll also feel refreshed and confident almost immediately.

So if you're really looking to think out of the box, start by doing something you normally wouldn't do in the first place.

Chapter 8: Conduct Manifestation Experiments

Once you've developed a basic premise for a growth mindset, it's now time to conduct manifestation experiments. But what is a manifestation experiment and how does it work? Well, for starters, this experiment is all about following a series of steps to achieve the goal you want to accomplish. And yes, you need to do this even after stimulating your creative prowess, reinforcing your knowledge, and setting a basic premise for your growth mindset.

I personally vouch for this experiment as I've already tried it, and the results have been pretty good. Following my success, I urged a couple of my friends to try the activity, and almost everybody had good things to say about it. Here's what you need to do.

7-Step Manifestation Experiment

As evident from the title, this seven-step manifestation experiment deals with seven different things that you're required to do for a week. Once you complete these steps, you're a step ahead of accomplishing your specific manifestation goal.

What Will You Need for This Experiment?

While you won't need anything tangible during the experiment, the entire process requires you to be calm and patient. So once you prepare yourself by being a little patient, you can immediately start out with the experiment. In the next sections, we'll discuss the seven different activities that you need to try for seven different days. Once you try all these activities, you will end up achieving success just like you've always wanted.

Day One: Choose Your Goal

This is the first step of our seven-day manifestation experiment. As you can already guess from the title, this step requires you to choose a specific goal. Now, while we all know that you want to be successful and that alone is your primary goal, the deal here is to choose something small. Like we've already discussed, success is not something that you can achieve overnight. You need to struggle, strive, and work really hard to achieve everything you've always dreamed of. So in order for this experiment to work, it is always better to go with something small. Do note that, despite being small, this should be something that you actually want. It should be something that truly lights you up and is compatible with your final plan of being successful.

This can be anything ranging from your office assignment to the upcoming exam you have at your university. It's important to choose something you really want because that alone will keep you driven and passionate throughout the week. Since you can only achieve a goal if you're truly passionate, this is a must. Because this book is about success and developing a successful mindset, we'll assume that your goal is to complete an assignment by the end of the following week. This assignment is really important to your career, as it might result in a possible raise. However, since it's time sensitive, you're slightly wary about getting it done.

Once you've chosen your goal, jot it down on paper. While many people choose not to write their goals down, such is not the case with our experiment. Since this experiment needs you to be absolutely focused, you need write down your goal on this paper.

Day Two: Make a List of Positive Affirmations

Affirmations play a vital role in helping you unlock success. It is these affirmations, backed by proper techniques and insight, that truly help you in creating the kind of life you want. Whether it's a sales professional, an entrepreneur, a best-selling author, or an award-winning athlete, affirmations work for almost everybody. And that is exactly why our second step deals with making a list of positive affirmations. Before making these affirmations, get rid of all negative thoughts as they play a detrimental role in helping you carry out the manifestation experiment.

Now that everything else is on track, it's high time you start with the affirmation. For this, you will have to write down the things that you want to happen. Since our experiment is about using your manifesting power to complete your work by the end of next week, you can use the following sets of affirmations:

- "I will successfully complete my work by the (enter date) of next week."

- "The task is difficult, but I have the capability to achieve it. I will achieve my task."

- "I will allocate three hours a day to focusing

entirely on the task."

- "The task is challenging, but I will accomplish it."

- "I will conquer every roadblock that comes my way."

- "I will strive to achieve my goal, undeterred."

Remember, your daily affirmations are to your mind what exercise is to your body. So writing these affirmations down, and repeating them, will help you in reprograming your subconscious mind. It will also help you in achieving your manifestation power.

Affirmations, when used the right way, significantly reduce all negative beliefs that tend to limit you. It is these affirmations that'll transform you from your current state of comfort and help you walk towards a more expanded realm. It will ensure that no belief or thought process can limit your potential or dampen your spirit. None of us want to be stuck in mediocrity, and this is exactly why you need to try these affirmations. When carried out the right way, they will help you in transforming the "I can't" into "I can." And by the time you complete this experiment, you will be way beyond your fears, uncertainties, and doubts.

Day Three: Try Active Visualization

After you've successfully sailed through the first and the second day, it's now time to try something more substantial: creative visualization. Creative visualization goes a long way in helping you achieve your final goal. It also has an equally important role in helping you use your inherent power of manifestation. But what exactly does visualization deal with? Well, the idea is pretty simple. Here, all you need to do is build a clear, concrete picture about the kind of things that are going to happen as you start manifesting.

In order for this experiment to work out successfully, it's advisable to use a vision board.

This small whiteboard will feature your thoughts and insights about the manifestation process. Here, you will have the freedom to follow any and every approach you deem fit. So whether you're looking to convey your thoughts through words, pictures, cartoons, or any other visual representation, everything will work as long as it somehow represents your goals. In case you haven't seen a visualization board, and don't know how it works, try a simple Google search for better insight.

Once you jot down some stuff on this visualization

board, turn your attention to the specific areas that you've written about. Relax for a while and then start analyzing these areas as if they're in your current, existing reality. What exactly are you scared about in this manifestation process? What do you think will prevent you from achieving the manifestation successfully? Is it fear, apprehension, or anything else? Continue this exercise until you have a list of everything which you think holds the power of limiting your abilities.

Day Four: Try the 'as If' Game

The fourth day of your experiment deals with the 'as if' game. The idea of this game is pretty simple. All you need to do is act as if the things you're dreaming of are eventually going to come true. Also known as 'living in the knowing,' this 'as if' game helps you build a positive mindset which is imperative to the success of your final goal. You can also team it with positive visualization and positive affirmations for a more lasting impact.

So if you're looking to achieve the task at hand by the end of the coming week, believe that you've already achieved it. Think about the various steps that you've taken to achieve this goal and as you do this, try manifesting these steps in actual, real-time actions. For instance, if your job requires you to research a specific topic, visualize yourself researching it. As you see yourself doing this in your imagination, you will automatically feel a push to try it in reality. If the project also requires you to call some important people, make the phone calls in your imagination, and like the former exercise, this will compel you to get the ball rolling right away.

Similarly, if you want to be appreciated for the job you've done, try visualizing how it will feel to get appreciated. The words you hear will act as an automatic motivation that'll push you into completing the task and meeting your goal within your deadline. Although this might seem like escapism to some, many people have tried it, and the results have been amazing, to say the least. So all you need to do is act like you're already successful, and you'll soon find your day getting better and your confidence spiking like never before.

Day Five: Make a Gratitude List

When you finally reach the fifth day, think about things that are somewhat similar to the kind of things that you are looking to manifest. As you start visualizing these things, you have to specifically ensure that you already have these things in your life. Right after this, focus on the emotion of gratitude that is evoked because of the presence of these things.

Since our final goal is about getting your work done by the end of the week, you can list your assignments that have already been successful. Alternatively, you can also visualize those moments when you have been appreciated and congratulated for the work you've done. As you start thinking about these different things, they will end up acting as a boost to your current manifestation goals. Thinking about these things will remind you that you've been successful earlier on, and they, therefore, will reinforce the insight that this time, too, you will have the power and the capability of achieving success in your desired goal. Your manifestation potential alone will reach an entirely new level, and you will soon find an inherent power that will compel you to complete the task at hand.

If, however, you start getting a feeling as if you're struggling to achieve your manifestation goals, try checking the common mistakes that most people make while implementing these goals. You can also try online personalized tests if you find yourself stuck in a rut. These tests will conduct a detailed analysis and help you figure out the things that are holding you back. Since most online platforms conduct these tests, it'll also be easier for you to get them and follow them from scratch.

Day Six: Find the Right Opportunities

If you're looking to manifest something, you cannot just sit back and hope for it to happen. So the sixth day of this experiment involves proper, real-time action. Remember, you can only achieve success if you have an open-minded approach about your goals and inspirations. So do not let anything bog you down and do not be constrained by any potential, imaginary roadblocks. Remember, every roadblock comes with a solution and it is your responsibility to find the solution and use it to its maximum potential.

In this case, you're looking to complete a project in a tight deadline but cannot seem to find a way to do so. But that's not how the situation is. Well, not if you look at it the right way. All you have to do is look properly. If you're having time constraints, try to sit back and sketch out a plan to achieve your impending goal. Say, for instance, the deadline is within seven days and you have to finish the task before the assigned time. To make things worse, you already have a date and a doctor's appointment in the middle of the week. So what's a probable solution?

First things first; try to have a discussion with your partner and inform them about the importance of this project. In all likelihood, she or he will understand the situation and won't make an issue of it. Now to the doctor's assignment. This one, too, can be easily handled if you use the right strategies. Since you've booked the appointment and have already paid for it, try assigning yourself less work on that specific day. Divide your work into small parts and keep the smallest bit for the day of your appointment. This will make things simpler and you won't feel the load that would have otherwise bogged you down.

So all you have to do is fish for the right opportunities and seize them as soon as you can.

Day Seven: Share Your Results

Now that you've reached the final day of your goal, it's time to track your results. At this point, think about the things you've achieved during the experiment and try jotting them down on a piece of paper. Your experience might not have been entirely smooth. You might have faced little or big roadblocks along the way. But even then, don't hesitate to write about your experiences.

Be patient and uninhibited while writing your results. Do not be afraid to write down the littlest of details as they'll only help you figure out how you've actually performed in the exercise. Finally, when you're done writing down everything about the exercise, take some time to filter the content and highlight the goals you've achieved. This might not be the end goal that you had thought of in the beginning. It can also be something entirely different. But in order to complete the experiment successfully, it is really important that you write down your thoughts about the final process.

As you read what you've written down, try to reflect on the various steps that you took in order to finally reach your goal. These steps should be clear and completely detailed. Additionally, also make a section to jot down the lessons you've learned throughout the entire process. This should be pertaining to your final goal. Write about the snippets of wisdom you grasped while undertaking the mission to achieve this much coveted goal. Write about the thoughts you had during the process. When you finally read this piece of paper, you will be beyond thrilled to browse through the things that you've achieved along the way. It'll keep you satisfied and truly happy.

Chapter 9: Track Your Manifestation

Well, now that you've tried the manifestation experiment and every other guideline featured in this book, it's high time you track the success of your manifestation. In this chapter, we will discuss the signs that indicate whether or not you're a step closer to achieving your goal.

Why Do You Need to Track Your Manifestation?

When you're looking tap in the power of manifestation, you don't already know whether or not your goals will come to fruition. After all, the things you see around you might not be the perfect representation of the things you want. In fact, something entirely different and unexpected might be brewing in the backdrop, without your slightest knowledge.

While we can't really tell you the ideal time to manifest, we can share the signs that'll help you check if the manifestation experiment worked in your favor.

You Will Start Feeling Better

While this might not be the most satisfying answer, it's still a big clue since we manifest according to our emotions at the spur of the moment. So when you're feeling good, it is most possibly because you are aligning with everything that you've always wanted.

It is our state of mind and our emotions that end up determining everything happening in our lives. So when you feel better about achieving the things you want to, it automatically means that the resistance is reduced and trust is developed; both of which collectively indicate a successful manifestation experiment.

Although you might not feel amazing or perfectly in sync with the world every single time that is not a problem because, after a while, you will definitely start getting a proper grasp of your inherent thought process.

Always remember, you want the things you're looking to achieve because you want to experience a specific kind of feeling. So if you're anywhere close to that feeling right now, you are undoubtedly thinking the right kinds of thoughts and doing the right kinds of things.

Your journey alone is what your goal is truly about, and the entire process of achieving your goal is exciting to say the least. So if you're feeling good about yourself and about your goals, the destination is pretty near.

The key here is to be completely patient without getting attached to specific results. You should also train yourself to avoid brooding about the ways in which you think you're going to achieve your goals.

You Will Start Having Plenty of Dreams

Very often, our dreams don't really make that much sense. After all, they are nothing but our subconscious mind and a couple of trapped collective images. It is these images that later pop out all of a sudden, giving us every kind of thought.

But if you notice carefully, you will find a pattern in your dreams. I always end up dreaming about good things, right before something good is about to happen in my life. So all I'm suggesting you to do right now is consider the possibilities of using this exercise.

According to a study, we sleep for around one-third of our lives. So even before you get to bed, start conjuring the image of the thing that's attracting you. Once you do this, your subconscious will do the rest of the job for you. Since your dreams are a space for your subconscious mind, you can actually add anything you want in there. So if you suddenly wake up from your sleep, afraid of some random thing, it is nothing but your subconscious trying to trick you. Several psychologists also suggest that this is just your subconscious mind's defense mechanism where it tries to release any fear from you.

Luckily, your subconscious mind will also inform you if something good is about to happen. And this is exactly when you have those miraculous dreams about achieving your goals. So, when you start dreaming a bit too often about reaching and achieving your goals, consider it to be a pertinent sign because this clearly suggests that you're a step closer to achieving your manifestation goals.

As you start relaxing, and as you start trusting the world around you, your dreams will turn out to be more vibrant and real. Your subconscious mind is happy with the fact that you are taking care of your life, because this also indicates that you've chosen love over fear. So when you no longer find stress, anxiety, or restlessness in your dreams, that is your manifestation power doing its job.

You Will Be More in Sync with New People

Another significant way to track your goal is by checking whether you meet more likeminded people along the way. I've personally met several new people who've helped me achieve my final goal. Interestingly enough, I met them just at the point when I was stuck or in a complete rut. It was with their collective efforts that helped me end up meeting most of my goals. So if you experience the same thing, it is very likely that you're on the verge of meeting your final goal.

When you're truly in the right path of reaching your goal, you end up attracting plenty of resources who knowingly or unknowingly help you in meeting your goal. Alternatively, you also encounter several events that somehow offer positive indications about your goal. At this point, one of the best things to do is to say 'yes' to every new opportunity that comes along your way.

As you do this, you will automatically observe a greater flow in your energy. Interestingly, you will also have a fair share of miracles that'll start unfolding, giving you the proof that the manifestation exercise truly works in your favor.

You Will Experience a Sudden, Inexplicable Sense of Calm

This is yet another direct indicator that your manifestation experiment is working. Usually, when you're on a journey to achieve something, your mind is bogged down by fear, anxiety, and apprehension. You can't help but think about every possibility that might directly or indirectly jeopardize your goal.

But as you start making progress towards your goal, these thoughts of anxiety will automatically be replaced by a sense of calm. You will be relaxed and comfortable. Instead of being anxious and unhappy, you will do things at your own pace. You will tell yourself about taking inspired actions when they come to you in their own sweet time. You won't be thinking about the goal; it is the path and the journey that'll keep you hooked. You'll no longer worry and will instead take slow, steady, and confident steps towards meeting and achieving your goal.

Others won't understand this. They will ask you to work hard and complete everything almost immediately. But nothing will bother you anymore. Your deeper sense of calm will guide you and you will experience a positive energy throughout your journey. Every time someone reminds you about the complexity of your journey, you'll reassure them with your newfound insights. You will tell them that there's practically nothing to be worked up about and that you will indeed achieve your goal within your desired deadline.

When you start experiencing this deep sense of calm, every negativity, hate, doubt, roadblock, or challenge won't seem to be difficult anymore. Such will be your state of mind that nothing under the sun can bother you. Whether someone cuts you off on your way to work, or a random stress crops up, practically nothing will have the ability to tamper with your peace. You will be constantly reassured by the fact that everything is going well and success is coming your way.

Very often, people start worrying because they are addicted to the act of worrying in the first place. This is primarily because we assume that we have the power to control everything happening around us. So when you experience this sudden transition in consciousness, where you're no longer bothered about controlling everything, you might ask yourself— "Do I really care about these things anymore?"

Trust me, this is not because you don't care, but rather because of your newfound insights and knowledge. It is these inexplicable insights that will guide you. Interestingly enough, you won't be able to perfectly understand or articulate them. And this is exactly when you know you're heading towards success.

So every time you experience this sense of calm, always remember one thing—like a rearview mirror, your final goal is closer than it seems right now.

You Will Start Experiencing DéJà Vu

Have you ever experienced déjà vu moments? These are the moments where you feel like you've already been somewhere before. This can be a place where you always wanted to go, or a random place that you've never visited before. Alternatively, it can also be a situation where you see yourself achieving the goal you've always wanted to. The following day, amid your chores, you feel like something is about to happen—and lo and behold! You end up experiencing the exact same thing you saw in your dreams.

It is situations like these that indicate the good stuff that is likely to happen in your life. Remember, your life is nothing but a hologram built from the images programmed in your subconscious mind. So when the world starts giving you glimpses of the things that are likely to happen, there's a high possibility that these things will indeed happen within the next couple of days.

The things you experience in life are nothing but a projection of your inherent consciousness. So if you're having these déjà vu moments, it is only likely that you're right on the verge of something great that'll come into your life; you're on the verge of achieving something that you've been striving to accomplish.

So even if you feel like giving up, don't! You're almost on the edge of achieving your dreams. All you have to do is walk a few more steps.

Your Intuitive Abilities Will Be in Full Swing

When you're following the manifestation experiments and doing everything that needs to be done, your intuitive abilities will be elevated. You'll find several instances where you'll end up saying things right before someone else. You might also end up unknowingly doing things that the other person wants you to do. You'll have an inherent knowing that the current frequency of your reality is slowly and steadily moving up. Whether it's picking up your phone even before it rings, or unknowingly finding a space in the parking lot, there will be signs everywhere. All you need to do is look properly.

Chapter 10: Perform Active and Passive Affirmations

Affirmations are statements that are primarily designed to bring about a change in our lives. They can serve as an inspiration or reminder, helping you to do well in life. You can also use these active and passive affirmations to focus on the goals you've set throughout the day. When implemented the right way, they promote significant and sustained transformation that goes a long way in keeping you satisfied and happy. In this chapter, we will discuss the relevance advantages of these active and passive affirmations.

How to Write an Affirmation

Now that you know everything about the ways in which affirmations can transform you, you might be wondering whether you can write one in the first place. Writing affirmations is one of the easiest things that you will ever do. All you have to do is follow the instructions carefully. In this section, we list the instructions that'll help you in writing positive affirmations.

Always Write Your Affirmations in First Person

If you're planning to write affirmations, do so in first person. "I," "I will," and "I am" are ideally the kinds of statements that will transform your affirmations to the ultimate basis of your identity. These statements of identity can act as significantly powerful motivators for an impending change. Some of the best statements can be along the lines of "I am truly confident in speaking before people,"; "I have a goal and I will achieve it"; "I will complete my work by the end of next week"; "I am a compassionate individual."

Affirmations Are Always Written from a Positive Perspective

While writing affirmations, always make them positive. So instead of saying "I don't enjoy the smell/taste of cigarettes anymore," try saying something like "I am absolutely free from the confines of smoking" or "I am a healthy individual and I love my body when I start making healthy choices."

Affirmations Bring Forth an Emotional Transformation

When you're trying to use affirmations, also make it a point to add some feeling. Using emotional phrases in your affirmations is extremely important because of the significant relationship between emotions and your semantic experiences. So swap statements like "I spend a lot of time with my elderly parents" with more positive statements like "I get a strong feeling of gratitude while spending time with my mom and dad." Instead of writing "I only make healthy choices" try saying "I feel energetic and happy when I eat healthy stuff."

Affirmations Should Always Be Written in Your Current State

Another ground rule for writing affirmations is writing them as if they are already happening in your life. This alone is the primary goal of affirmation. So instead of writing "two months from now I'll be truly happy and satisfied" write something along the lines of "I am happy right now." Similarly, swap "I will be attractive when I lose eight pounds" with "I am attractive the way I am." Unless you take a step towards embracing positivity, nothing you do will make a relevant difference.

While this step might cause some of you to falter, as you might feel silly writing something that you don't really believe, remember: the very purpose behind these affirmations is to write what's within your subconscious mind. Unless you do this, you will always falter and be unable to achieve your goals.

According to several holistic traditions, the more you start acting like something is true, the more likely the chances for it to happen. So if you think you're attractive and beautiful, you will inadvertently associate yourself with the behaviors that will help you accomplish your goals.

In addition to following all these guidelines, avoid getting trapped in the 'how.' If you constantly weigh out options, think about the possibilities, and ponder the various ways in which a certain thing will happen, you will unknowingly create a sense of disbelief that'll get in the way of achieving your goal. However, if you are certain about your inherent ability of achieving the goal, you will subconsciously find a way of making it work in your favor.

Affirm your current achievements (or the things that you are consciously confident about) as they play a vital role in undercutting any possible dissonance. In addition to this, they also help you reinforce a sense of belief within your system.

Several healers also suggest you write your own affirmations instead of randomly picking them. When you write something down, it automatically reflects your deepest desires which help you to connect with your goal better. In addition to writing your affirmations down, we suggest you to update them from time to time. As humans, we are bound to change. So when you actually make the conscious effort to update your goals, their emotional potency significantly increases.

How to Make Your Affirmations Work

Your job doesn't end with writing a solid set of affirmations. Contrarily, that is just the beginning of your lifelong quest of achieving everything you want. In order to make your affirmations truly work, you will have to go by a set of rules. These rules will define your goal and help you achieve it sooner. But how do we even start out with making our affirmations work? Well, let's find out!

Step 1

As part of the first step, you will have to come up with a list of everything that you deem your negative traits. Here, you can add the criticisms that your friends have pointed out about you, or the gray shades of your character that make you feel ashamed. You can also add the stuff your parents, partners, or siblings said while you were still a child, or the things your boss told you during your last performance review. Do not weigh the accuracy of these statements. Do not analyze them. On the contrary, try accepting that everybody comes with flaws, and you are not an exception. In fact, the beauty of human existence is our ability to make flaws and rectify them when we come to know of them. So instead of brooding or harboring hate, try looking for a common theme. This can be anything pertaining to your behavior, habits, the way you talk, or anything else. But regardless of the flaw, make it a point to find out about it and write it down.

This is one of the best ways to start bringing about a transformation in your beliefs and your life. As you start writing down your recurring beliefs, try figuring out if you're holding onto the belief anywhere within your system. For instance, do you immediately feel a sense of dread when you try thinking about this flaw? Remember, if you are really looking to bring a positive change in your life, it is really important to recognize your flaw and work on it. So right after identifying the common theme, try observing or looking back on the way you behaved when someone pointed that flaw out to you.

Step 2

For the second step, you will have to write down the positive things about yourself. In case you're not really good with words, try using a thesaurus to find powerful, strong, and significant words that have the ability to transform you. So instead of saying "I am responsible," try saying something like "I am truly accountable for all my actions." Right after jotting down the affirmation, ask a friend or a colleague to have a look at it and add their suggestions. When you take more suggestions from people, you unknowingly make your affirmations stronger.

Step 3

Now that you've written it down, try speaking the affirmation loudly and clearly for at least five minutes at a time. Do this three times a day for best results. One of the best times to say this is while you're getting dressed for work, shaving, or doing your makeup because these are the moments when you look at yourself directly in the mirror.

In addition to doing this, we also suggest you write down this affirmation many times in your notebook. This will help in reinforcing a new kind of belief. Also, as you start writing down the things you want to express, you will notice a gradual but steady shift in the style of the narrative. This serves as an excellent clue about the way your mind perceives new concepts. You can call this task a mindfulness journal since it is driven by the primary agenda of ensuring positive affirmation.

Step 4

At this stage, try anchoring the affirmation in your system as you repeat it by keeping your hand on any specific area that went stiff when you jotted down your negative thoughts in the first place. It is also important to breathe into your affirmation while you say or write it. Once you start reprograming your mind with this exercise, you'll slowly want to shift from the concept of a mere affirmation to a more real, strong embodiment of the kind of quality you're seeking.

Step 5

Choose a friend or a coach who will repeat your affirmation and remind you to practice doing it. This is yet another significant way to ensure that the affirmation works. So when your friend says that "you are a wonderful person," try identifying and believing this message.

In case you don't have a friend who'll be comfortable doing this for you, try using your mirror reflection. Talk to reflection by reinforcing it with this healthy, motivating message.

Once you complete this step, there is a high possibility that your affirmation will start working. Remember, affirmations are powerful tools that help you in changing your current state of mind, so your mood manifests the kind of change you want to see in your life.

However, these affirmations will only work well when you finally identify the negative beliefs that are standing in their way of success. In case you don't find these suggestions work, try using a professional therapist who will help you unearth the thoughts that are buried deep down in your subconscious mind. You can also start a meditation practice for better results. As mentioned in the previous chapters, mindfulness meditation is one of the best ways to unearth the thought patterns that lie deep in your subconscious mind. It doesn't help you in categorizing them, but assists in identifying the aspects that are wholesome and the ones that are negative. Growth and success aren't about change; rather, they are about the ability to accept a reality and move undeterred towards your goal. So try this affirmation practice and witness your life changing right before your own eyes.

Chapter 11: Self-Guided Meditations for Manifestors

While in the previous chapters you learned quite a bit about the various manifestation experiments, in this chapter we will discuss self-guided meditations for manifestors. Self-guided meditation plays a vital role in helping you achieve a calm state of mind which is further conducive to achieving success. But how can you be patient during a meditation session? Are there any rules that you are required to follow? You will find every answer to your questions about meditation in this penultimate chapter.

How to Use Meditation for Achieving Your Manifestation Goals

Meditation is one of the simplest ways to achieve your goals pertaining to manifestation. And guess what? The exercises you're required to perform are easy, simple, and absolutely time-efficient. In case you're meditating for the first time and don't really know how to go forward, here's a detailed walkthrough that'll help you perform everything you're required to for achieving your manifestation goals.

Since these are extremely simple guidelines, you needn't worry even if you are a beginner. All you have to do is follow every individual step to ensure complete success in your goals.

Find Your Goal

Although the primary goal for any and every meditation is achieving inner peace, there are also a couple of short-term goals that you can achieve with this. So if you have a manifestation goal, use it for your meditation as well. Since this book is all about the guidelines to being successful, try specifically focusing on the goals that are related to short-term success. Like in the previous chapter, here we will use an example of a work assignment that needs to be submitted by the following week. You can always have any other goal. All you need to do is be focused on it.

Now that you have your goal at hand, start contemplating your life and thinking about the things that you need immediately. In addition to the completion of your assignment, this can also be related to health, your emotional needs, your psychological needs, your performance in relationships, and so on.

Address the Needs You Have Right Now

Just like achieving physical fitness deals with a structured learning pattern, you'll also find a similarly structured pattern for your inherent peace and spiritual well-being. If you are looking to use this manifestation exercise to be successful in life, you first have to start out by clearing all doubts and anxieties from your mind.

The ability to empty your mind is the indication of a truly mature meditative practice. The important thing here is to be completely practical and focus on your short-term goals, despite having bigger and better aspirations. This alone will set your path in complete motion. Since it takes some time for developing your inner skills, you need to completely prepare yourself for developing a quiet state of mind. If you start the meditation with an idea that you won't be able to empty your mind, you will be disillusioned throughout the practice.

Fix the Time and Spot of Your Meditation

Very often, people assume that meditation for extensive periods of time is the only way of achieving anything valuable. But this is nothing but a myth. You can achieve everything you want in life even with a few minutes of meditation on a daily basis. This will not just give you better results but will also help you in staying consistent with your goals.

To begin with, you have to be kind with yourself. Avoid imposing irrelevant, stringent, and unrealistic strictures. Come up with a meditation program that is not just flexible but also equally creative. For instance, you can always use alternative meditative practices on alternate days of the week.

In case you can only spare a few minutes during the day, take that time to reflect on the things you do. This act of connecting your body and mind with your own awareness is an extremely powerful practice that can nourish and heal you to the core.

Follow the Right Steps

Now that every other thing is in place, it is high time you start with the practice. However, before you start, make it a point to follow each and every step carefully. In this section, we provide details about every individual step that you're required to follow for your manifestation meditation.

Sit Comfortably – For the first step, sit in a

comfortable position. This can be anywhere ranging from your home, workplace, car, to a friend's home or anywhere else. All you need to do is find this place, make yourself comfortable, and gently place your hands right above your lap. Make sure you don't close your eyes during the process. You can also use a specific position by placing the back of your hand on your knees while connecting the thumb and index finger of both your hands.

Recognize Your Feelings – In this step you will start recognizing your feelings. We particularly suggest you recognize the negative emotions or the feelings that are floating along your mind or body. Locate the exact point where you experience the sense of negativity in your system and start observing it in a non-judgmental way. Let this feeling persist and understand that it is absolutely normal to experience negative thoughts.

Start Breathing – Now that you've completed the first two steps, try focusing on breaths. Do this for a while and then change the tempo of your breaths to slow, deep ones. Feel your breath making its way to your nose, all along your throat, within your chest, and down by your abdomen. You will find it swirling back right out of your mouth. Try feeling the breath in your body and observing it as it reaches you and escapes you effortlessly.

Start feeling – For the following step, focus on your feelings, because it is these feelings that'll guide you towards success. To start this process, try breathing while you focus on the specific part of the body which exudes negative energies. For instance, if you feel a sense of anxiety or stress along your chest, try taking deep breaths and observing the way your chest responds to the process.

As you do this, the discomfort will persist for a while, but do it anyway. Why? Because, very often, it is useful to welcome negative feelings with the 'bring it on' approach. Do not be wary of accepting challenges; rather, allow yourself to be confident enough to fight them.

Try Focusing Better – Every time your mind starts wandering, allow it to focus on your breath. Try hearing the normal sound of your breath and feeling the sensations as they enter and leave your body. It is absolutely normal to have several thoughts clouding your mind while you're trying to work with the meditation. There's nothing wrong with this, so let those thoughts be here. All you have to do is carefully observe them without any judgment.

One of the best ways to handle your thoughts during the meditation is by recognizing them, accepting their presence, sitting with them for a while, and finally, releasing them. By the time you release these thoughts, you can actually picture them like small clouds floating across the sky.

Live The Moment – For the final step, just be. Continue breathing, observe your breaths, and try feeling how your body reacts to these sensations. Try accepting your negative feelings and watch them while they try to come and go. Once you practice this, you will be much more accepting and confident about the things that life throws in your way.

Follow the Correct Posture

When you are meditating, it is also extremely important to follow the right posture. In this section, you will find a set of steps that will help you correct your posture and perform your meditation more effectively.

Keep Your Back Straight - When you are meditating, it is really important to sit in an upright position where your back is completely straight. For instance, if you are sitting on a chair, do not slouch and keep your back completely erect. This posture will help you stay alert and it will also allow you to focus on your breath more easily.

Do Not Blink - When you are meditating, you should either keep your eyes closed or open. Since the goal of meditation is to boost your attention muscles, blinking will affect your concentration and keep your mind diverted. If you find it more comfortable to concentrate when your eyes are closed, try keeping them completely closed. Contrarily if you are tired and have a habit of dozing off with closed eyes, keep your eyes slightly open and focus your gaze on a soft space. This space can be a wall, the floor, a chair or any other object.

Do not fidget with your hands - While some people claim that using thumb movement ensures better concentration, it is really not a necessary part of meditation. Ideally, you should rest your hands, and place your palm down on your legs. However, you can always follow any other hand posture that makes you feel comfortable.

Cross Your Legs in Your Preferred Position - When you're meditating, you can comfortably cross your legs while keeping your back upright. However, there isn't any hard-and-fast rule to this. If you feel more comfortable in folding your feet, try doing that for more comfort and better concentration.

Bend Your Head Slightly Downward - Even when your eyes are closed, it is really important to bend your head downwards. This will offer added comfort during meditation. However, as you do this, please ensure that your back is completely upright.

The main idea of meditation is to find a posture that isn't just comfortable but also keeps you upright. These guidelines work for several people and there's a high possibility that they'll work for you as well. An extremely comfortable meditative pose will make you sleepy, and the least comfortable posture will keep you distracted. So it is always better to find a pose that has a proper balance of comfort and support.

Connect with Your Spirit Guides

Once you're well-versed with the tips that'll make your meditation successful, it is time to try something else. In case you haven't guessed from the title already, in this section, we are going to discuss connecting with your spirit guides. This is a simple meditative exercise that will reinforce the positive spirit in your system and help you aim higher. Once you practice this from time to time, you'll end up creating the necessary mindset for reaching your goals pertaining to success.

But what exactly are these spirit guides? Well, spirit guides are the ethereal beings who are connected to you even before you're born. These guides alert and guide you throughout your life. Many people connect with their guides for fulfilling the spiritual contract that they had already made before incarnation. Your higher selves will assist you in choosing these guides who will eventually help you, alert you, and render intuitive insight within you. Some of these spirit guides will spend your entire life with you, while others will come up at specific times to help you achieve your life goals. They either guide you individually, or assist a group/panel of other people along with you.

While guiding you, these spirit guides incite energy within your soul and give you the proper direction to fulfill and achieve your earthly goals. Did you know that you can connect with your spirit guides whenever you desire? Isn't it comforting to know that you have someone by your side when you need proper direction and guidance? This script has assisted a lot of my clients and I love it for its simplicity and effectiveness. But before you get started with it, trust yourself completely and weed out your ego. Follow the techniques well, and practice the script patiently.

A Complete Guide to Connect with Your Spirit Guides

Choose a quiet and calm place for meditation.

Relax for a few minutes and close your eyes.

Now, slowly, try to meditate. While meditating, imagine a happy place. This happy place can be your home, your bed, a beach, or anywhere else where you feel happy.

Be completely focused on your thoughts.

Be patient and give yourself ample time to meditate.

Breathe deeply, settle your mind, and be completely calm.

Once you get to a clear and calm state, start summoning your spirit guide. Try to picture the image of your spirit guide.

It may not have a proper shape and appearance. It can be a bubble of thoughts ... A face ... A person you love, or an entirely new person whom you've never seen before ... Feel their presence ... Feel the presence of the guiding force around you.

Now, gently ask the name of your spirit guide. Concentrate. You will hear someone whispering, "I am Martin" or "I am Zora."

If you cannot hear a name, don't worry. Your guide may want you to give him/her a name. Greet them with any name you want. Call them "Harmony," "Ecstasy," "Faith," or any other name that you see fit.

Start communicating with your spirit guides. Remember, they are spirits meant to help you succeed in your goals so you cannot hide anything from them. Be completely honest. Don't be shy or scared to share your thoughts with them. Pour your heart out. Tell them all that you want.

Continue to sit in complete silence until your spirit guides answer you.

You will hear an answer to your thoughts and questions. You might hear faint whispers like "you can do it" or "you already know the answer to this."

Your spirit guides may also choose to communicate with you in a mode other than words. They can communicate through pictures, memories, and symbols.

At this point, several things will come to your mind randomly and you have to pay particular attention to the things that repeat and connect you to your questions and thoughts. You will receive crystal-clear messages in the form of song lines, lines from movies and books, and lines from conversations you've had with friends and acquaintances.

Continue to meditate and demonstrate your faith and

belief in the existence of the spirit guide. Cultivate a close and deep relationship with your guide by communicating with them with your full concentration.

As your questions are gradually answered, you will soon feel your guide inciting a sense of energy within you. Right after this, you will feel a strong and powerful presence of an added energy and a higher vibration every time you manifest your special gifts or talents.

Be happy and smile, knowing that your spirit guide can be called upon whenever you need help and guidance.

Affirmation – I release all feelings of negativity and embrace the gift of positive energy from my spirit guide.

When you practice this meditative exercise from time to time, you automatically take a step ahead toward reaching your goals pertaining to manifestation.

Chapter 12: Build Positive Expectations

There are innumerable things happening around us that can affect our moods. This is even more relevant if you are a sensitive person. But at some point in time, you have to realize that there's no point in thinking about the things that you cannot change. After all, what's the point in brooding about something that you can never influence? What's the point in lingering on things where you don't have any control? Why worry when worrying about something will not change its original course?

There are innumerable things to worry about. Whether it is next week's presentation or your kid's test results, something or other will always keep you anxious and worked up. But you have to change these thoughts if you want to attain success. In order to be truly successful in life, you have to shun that cloak of anxiety and embrace positivity instead. This will not just reduce your stress but will also take you with a step closer to attaining true success and contentment. Shunning anxiety and stopping worry will also help you attain mindfulness in the long run.

So stop yourself from these unnecessary broodings right away. Once you do this, you will be automatically relieved from the huge stress and anxiety that keeps you worked up. You will feel like some huge weight has been lifted from your shoulders. You will feel light and happy. And this is exactly what being successful is all about. This is exactly what finding peace is all about.

While shunning the thoughts of the past, you've also got to teach yourself about hoping for good things. Hope is something that we should never lose. But despite knowing its impact, we end up losing hope every time something doesn't work in our favor. We get extremely overwhelmed with our problems and forget that good things can also happen. We forget that the sun can always shine after a rainy and windy day. We take our troubles too seriously and fail to understand that these problems are mere bumps that'll be followed by sunshine and success.

Losing hope won't lead you anywhere. It is hope that drives our life. It is hope that teaches us the meaning of life. So start embracing hope. Start thinking about everything good that will eventually make its way to your life. Try to understand that your troublesome times are not forever. They are merely a part of your life that will only pass with time.

I find an innate sense of peace in knowing that, no matter whatever bad happens in my life, it'll pass. I have learned to realize that pain and suffering in life are temporal, and with time, things will be absolutely fine. This idea of things turning out to be absolutely fine helps me get rid of my negativity. With this hope, I feel better almost instantly.

So if you, too, get worked up with the trials, tribulations, and failures of your life, the best option is to get rid of this negativity. Reinforce your mind with a new hope and you will soon end up enjoying the best life has to offer.

In this chapter, I will discuss hope and the impact of positive expectations in our final goal of achieving success. Here, you will learn how simple, positive thoughts can change your entire perspective on life and be conducive to helping you accomplish your goals.

Building Positive Expectations

As discussed in the previous chapters, positivity is a state of mind. You alone have the power of influencing it. But how can you stay positive in the face of challenging situations? What are the steps that'll help you achieve your goal? Here are some guidelines that'll definitely help you find an answer to your questions.

Positive Affirmations

Although we have discussed this in the previous chapters, we will once more stress the impact of these affirmations in the final chapter. The idea here is to embrace a positive state of being. This means you will speak positively, work positively, and act positively. And one of the best ways to control your inherent dialogues and change them to positive ones is with affirmations that are written on a positive note.

Start out by saying "I will achieve this goal"; "I love myself and I know I can do it"; "I feel great and I will do it"; or "I am smart, confident and responsible.

Around 95 percent of your internal thoughts are determined by the manner in which you communicate with yourself throughout the day. Sadly enough, you usually do not talk to yourself in a positive, constructive, and happy way. It is almost as if you switch to your self-loathing attitude by default. It is almost as if you can't control yourself from thinking about the things that'll affect your emotional peace, lower your inherent self-esteem by a notch, or keep you worried and anxious about the future.

Since your mind is nothing but a garden, you have to

consciously assume the role of planting flowers and tending them carefully. Do not encourage weeds to grow in the beautiful garden of your mind. Shun the negative beliefs and keep your hopes alive with positive affirmations.

Visualization

Like positive affirmations, we have also stressed the importance of positive visualization in the previous chapters. Remember, perhaps your strongest ability is the fact that you have the strength to visualize and observe your goals as if you've already accomplished them. So create an intriguing picture of your impending goal, and try replaying this in your mind. As you do this from time to time, you will soon observe a sense of motivation that will drive you to work towards the goal.

Remember, your life will only be improved if your mental pictures are improved. So if you see yourself as a happy and successful person inside, the same will be reflected outside.

Surround Yourself with Positive People

If you're really looking to build positive expectations, yet another thing that you have to do is surround yourself with happy and positive people. Remember, it is your choice that truly has the power to make a difference. So if you live and associate yourself with positive people, they will automatically have a positive impact on your emotions and the expectations you have about your goal. Say, for instance, you have a friend who constantly finds something negative in almost everything you do or say. And even if you share the happiest moments of your life, they have something negative to say about it. Interestingly, there's also another friend who tries to see a silver lining in everything that comes their way. Even if they're late to work or in the middle of some mishap, they find a way to cheer up with a happy, positive thought. Now, who do you want to associate with? In all probability, you want the happy, positive person in your life as they can unknowingly motivate you to achieve your goal.

And this is exactly the reason why you need to interact with winners, positive individuals, and others who are inherently optimistic about life. Negative people will be the primary source of your unhappiness. So avoid those people at every turn. Promise yourself that you'll no longer be or associate yourself with people who have a negative or stressful impact on your life.

Devour Some Positive Mental Meals

Just like your body is healthy because you eat nutritious foods, your mind will be healthy when you feed it with the necessary mental protein. If you are looking to develop positive expectations about your goals, try replacing mental candy with mental protein. But what exactly is this mental protein? Well, this is nothing other than the insightful books, articles, and journals. This is nothing but the inspirational videos you watch.

So try feeding your mind with information and ideas that won't just uplift you but will also make you happier and more confident to a certain degree. Yet another simple way to do this is by listening to positive audio programs and insightful podcasts. Try feeding your mind constantly with all sorts of positive messages which you feel might help you act better by making you more capable in your specific domain.

When you actually take the initiative to watch these insightful things, they unknowingly have an impact on your subconscious. This, in turn, makes it easier for you to build positive expectations.

Positive Training

Almost everyone around us started off with some limited resources. Some people even started without any money in the first place. With time, their fortunes reversed and they soon got to achieve everything they always wanted in life. If you notice carefully, you'll find that most people who are now at the topmost rung of the societal or cultural ladder started from the bottom.

So how did they manage to change their fortune? Well, they did it by embarking on a path of lifelong learning and inherent development that eventually helped them reap riches from mere rags. With the right training and development, they achieved affluence from poverty and achievement from severe failures.

Always remember, while formal education will give you a job, it is only individual training and development that will help you achieve a fortune. So when you make the efforts to better your thoughts and actions, you end up taking better control of your life, thereby increasing the speed at which you're likely to move forward.

Law of Attraction

Following the law of attraction is yet another powerful technique that will help you to become a positive person. If you follow it in a correct way, this technique will bring about positive outcomes that have the power to make your life better.

The law of attraction will transform your expectations to self-fulfilling prophecies. So when you follow this, you will soon be able to achieve everything in life. All you need to do is embrace positivity and be confident in your endeavors. Once you do this, everything you want to achieve will be simpler and easier. Remember, you alone have the power to control your expectations. So it always better to expect good outcomes.

Expect to achieve your goals. Expect to be successful. Expect to be popular around new people and you will soon achieve everything you looked forward to.

Conclusion

Now that we've reached the end of the book, you've grasped some valuable insights about being successful. Throughout this book, we've explained the various steps towards achieving success. We've specifically focused on the growth mindset because we want you to understand the relevance of tirelessly striving to achieve a goal. We have also added some valuable insights pertaining to meditation and manifestation, both of which will collectively help you in accomplishing your goals.

Since we've reached the end of the book, we'd like to reiterate something: *never stop*. Regardless of the roadblocks, challenges, and trials you face along the way- you should always strive to achieve your goal.

Be focused, be positive, and follow a solid routine. Do not let your mind conjure images of the future. Instead, teach it to focus on the current moment and on your current goals. Remember, success is about focusing on your present and giving your all to make it better. So if you're really looking to be successful, focus on being committed, seek knowledge, and make your journey enjoyable.

As you try the meditation and manifestation exercises,

understand that the very process of embracing a change takes time. In fact, nothing about being successful is instantaneous. And this is exactly why you can't expect an overnight change. In order to truly make things work in your favor, you will have to be strong, growth-oriented, and patient. You need to give yourself the time for syncing with the new exercises and the new way of life.

While this might seem like a never-ending process in the beginning, such is not the case. Once you start following these guidelines, every new habit you learn will become a part of your success-driven lifestyle. So instead of wasting your time anymore, start working on your 'now' right away. We're pretty sure you'll manage to be successful just the way you want to! Good luck!

www.ingramcontent.com/pod-product-compliance
Lightning Source LLC
Chambersburg PA
CBHW070110080526
44586CB00013B/1248